motherhood to otherhood

motherhood to otherhood

STEP UP TO A NEW YOU

Use the Lessons Learned as a Mom
to Create Your New Life

by JULIA ROBERTS

founder of www.unpregnancy.com

RUNNING PRESS
PHILADELPHIA · LONDON

9 8 7 6 5 4 3 2 1
Digit on the right indicates the number of this printing

Library of Congress Control Number: 2007943491

ISBN: 978-0-7624-2957-8

The stories in this book represent real mothers and their experiences. In most cases, names and circumstances are changed to protect their privacy.

Running Press Book Publishers
2300 Chestnut Street
Philadelphia, PA 19103-4371

Visit us on the web!
www.runningpress.com

To my mother—whose pregnancy gave me life,
and whose ambition and vitality helped me
reach for Otherhood.

contents

who should read this book

When a woman has a baby, it's as if she were cut in two. —GLENN CLOSE

Motherhood to Otherhood introduces a new way to integrate your many selves, despite the demands and emotional tug of Motherhood, and get yourself to Otherhood – that long abandoned dream, that career you once cherished, the life you *want*.

    Motherhood to Otherhood introduces Unpregnancy – a life-change strategy for moms of all ages and stages. Unpregnancy reclaims the lessons you learned in pregnancy, birth and motherhood to help make your Otherhood a reality.

Just as pregnancy leads to Motherhood, Unpregnancy leads to Otherhood.

- This is not a parenting advice book, nor is it intended for mothers-to-be or newborn mothers (who, face it, don't have time to read anyway).
- **It is the perfect Mother's Day gift** for yourself, your mother, your friend, your aunt and your sister – as a thank you for being a mom, and as an opportunity to use that experience to get to her Otherhood.
- **It is for mothers who ask "what next?" and for mothers who say "what about me?"** Whether your last child was born two or 20 years ago, this book is for you. Many of us feel real birth pangs when we send our youngest off to kindergarten. For others, it's when the kids leave for college. *It's time to get a life.*
- **Some of us face our thirtieth, fortieth or fiftieth birthdays and suddenly realize we forgot about *our own* needs and dreams.** Motherhood is such a full-bodied experience that no part of our being —spiritual or physical—is not tapped, tried or pressed into action on behalf of our children. Now, do you believe your own dreams can come true?
- **Sometimes a big life event like disease, divorce, or losing a job can serve as a powerful wake-up call.**

Motherhood to Otherhood is for you, and all the mothers you know who'd like to indulge their own desires and dreams, and use a model from their own life experiences—pregnancy and motherhood—to create a great new life. Otherhood awaits…

introduction

When the doorbell rang, I indulged in one moment's nervousness and then responded. Ten women were due that morning to begin a nine-week seminar with me as host and lecturer. I had sent each woman my odd invitation to share the seminar and launch her own Unpregnancy. These were all people I knew, though not necessarily well, but who didn't know each other. And *none* of them knew what to expect of Unpregnancy. They were uneasy. I was panicky. I was going to talk about my new idea and ask women to work on their lives together—a risky business.

I was amazed and pleased as we settled in and got down to the subject at hand. As the women introduced themselves to each other, there was a palpable anxiety among us. It is hard, even among friends, to admit that you want more.

As mothers we are blessed. We share our lives with people we love and who love us in return. In this group we were doubly blessed since we were all seemingly happily married, educated, middle-class women.

Still, we were all there because we wanted to be more than just somebody's mom. How greedy would that seem? How needy would we appear? How distasteful is the mother who complains about having to make dinner, change diapers, read bedtime stories, indulge teenage rantings, drive 'tweens all over town or take an extra job to pay for her kid's college? Even when we get a thank-you, it doesn't give us back our time, energy, or opportunity to do something for ourselves.

But that's why we were all there—not just to complain, but to do something about it. To get more and to get back a sense of self we'd lost years ago. (Like the perennially lost sneaker: if we keep looking, will we find it? Tucked inside the couch? In the corner of the coat closet?)

In the throes of giving birth, I think we all lose our empowered, enlightened selves. Our minds are wiped clean of all expectation and we begin anew. Our bodies are shaken first by the need to survive and second by the need to protect and nurture our young. These two strong instincts drive the woman who was out of the mother-to-be. To find her again can be nearly impossible.

Maybe it's as simple as the advice we give toddlers looking for the misplaced sneaker: *Go back to where you last remember seeing it.* I retraced my steps to pregnancy to find my lost self.

This is how I introduced Unpregnancy to the assembled group. If we go back to the lessons and reality of our pregnancies, we will find what we want—more.

As our first session progressed, it was easy to share pregnancy remembrances and intimate labor and delivery stories. These tales rolled off the tongue even when they included lewd gestures or entailed admitting you'd been awful to your husband or an innocent bystander. We could honestly and easily share our feelings from that day so long before and so different for each of us. Among us we had 33 kids ranging in age from 2 to 19.

However, when it came to telling our dreams we were shy and awkward. It's hard to tell someone what you hope for. It is your best-kept secret. But we persevered, talking about Unpregnancy and what it meant for each of us. We wowed ourselves and each other as we dared to articulate what we wished we had become or dared to hope we could become now—a restaurateur, a real estate entrepreneur, a documentary filmmaker, a charitable fund administrator, a renowned architect, a PhD in speech pathology, a jeweler, and an author of a self-help book. We gasped. Until that moment, we had known each other only as playground moms.

The thing that surprised me was the relief and joy in the room. We had admitted to wanting something for ourselves. We had seen that this was hard for every other mother in the room. We had come out of isolation, the isolation that kept our hopes at bay, that whittled away our sense of deserving. We each stayed submerged in others' needs, not seeing to our own, not acknowledging how far we had sublimated our feelings, not wishing for ourselves, not thinking it was possible to escape.

But now we had briefly come out of isolation, spoken our true aspirations and enjoyed the shared validation—the right to our dreams. We experienced a brief, giddy sense of childish pleasure. But then we quickly shifted gears and returned to our normal roles. Realities returned to our consciousness. We all had too many obligations: kids, husbands, jobs, babysitters, volunteer work, parents to care for. Knowing that family logistics can be a true nightmare, we commiserated about the obstacles.

Peggy, one of the women in our group that day, was a mother of four (ages three to nine) who also cared for her own mother, who had MS. On top of that, Peggy had just moved her 90-year-old grandmother into their house because she needed round-the-clock supervision and Peggy hoped that having her at home would make life easier. Peggy "kept herself sane" by serving as president of her parent-teacher organization. Needless to say, she was overwhelmed. "It is kind of working," she said, as we all stared in disbelief. Peggy isn't a saint; she's just a woman trying to do what she thought was right for everyone who needed her (and sacrificing herself in the process).

Admittedly, a mother has no time. But remember the adage that says, if you want something done, ask a busy person. So ask yourself now what you want today. What can you do today to move toward that dream? Where are you planning and hoping to take your life? Where did you put your old ambitious, centered self? How can you get her back?

It is Peggy who helped me see a one-day-at-a-time strategy. With all her obligations, even she had faith that she could take small steps to claim her time and space and find herself and her passion using Unpregnancy. Before she left the group that day, Peggy shared one of her grandmother's aphorisms: "Treat today as the present it is meant to be."

introducing unpregnancy

Unpregnancy is a life-change strategy that will help you to conceive, protect, grow, and give birth to a new you. What are you doing for the next nine months? Time to make your life yours again.

What do you remember about pregnancy? I remember waking up in the middle of the night with numbingly painful spasms in my calves (talk about a rude awakening). With one pregnancy I had high blood pressure; I could barely walk a single block and that made it nearly impossible to get to work. I never really had morning sickness, for which I should be grateful. And though my feet did grow a full size larger, laying waste to a closet full of great shoes, my ankles didn't swell. Yes, thank goodness I retained my slim wrists and ankles which helped me delude myself into believing that my former body was still in there somewhere.

For me, pregnancy was a long time ago. And believe me, I'm not one of those people who romanticizes it. I didn't feel like Queen for a Day or buy into the idea that all pregnant women are so beautiful. (I subscribe to a much more cynical theory: maternity "fashions," waddling and exhaustion make most pregnant women look like Godzilla. "You're beautiful" is code for "It'll be over soon.")

For me, pregnancy was an annoying list of symptoms, each taking me completely by surprise, each out of my control, and each private and some-what humiliating. I was floored by the doctor's expectation that I could sim-ply postpone my life and spend months in bed to reduce stress when I had high blood pressure. (Without a salary, I would have lost my house, but no worries!) I remember feeling depressed when I accidentally caught a glimpse of my moon pie face in a mirror. And each of these belittling, painful, some-times terrifying symptoms was outmatched by mental and emotional symp-toms—forgetfulness, weepiness, the urge to nest.

All in all, I did not feel like *myself*. (I am not a "nester.") Despite my con-viction that someone had hijacked my body, pregnancy wasn't all bad; in fact, it quietly offered a gift—a healthy baby, which is of course the greatest gift of all. The new child in your life makes it all worth it. But there was another, qui-eter gift (a sleeper, you might say). This gift is the basis for Unpregnancy.

No matter what your list of symptoms, personal circumstances, or the size of your butt at its biggest, I know that at some time during pregnancy you felt it: awe and wonder, pride, a sense of purpose, a commitment to do everything right, or at least to do your very best. We came to understand what our bodies were meant to do and saw for ourselves what we could endure and achieve. And with the birth of our kids, we each changed our lives forever.

During each pregnancy, I came to understand what a mighty and righteous woman I am, *with the power to give life.* Super Mom! Then, *Bam!* My water broke and a baby arrived bearing the cutest combination of my husband's and my features and that glimpse of power evaporated. It was days before I had the power to sit comfortably, weeks before I regained the power to pull a comb through my hair, and years before I understood that, yes, I had come very close to unlocking my superpowers only to be foiled once again by Super Newborn! (Able to mesmerize fully grown adults wearing only diaper and cape—which looked suspiciously like a baby blanket) When my third and youngest child was three and I was bumping up against 40, I knew my biological alarm clock was ringing and I couldn't just keep hitting the snooze button. I had always wanted four children and it was now or never. I come from a large family and I really wanted four children, but there was no good rationale for a fourth child: we were a happy, busy family, approaching potty training on our last kid and ready to put away sippy cups forever. My husband was not in favor of a fourth.

I began to make a list of pros and cons, a task that initiated months of vacillating. Professionally, it wasn't a great time for me to have a baby. In addition, our then babysitter was pregnant, and I envied her. Her future was certain: she was having a baby and putting all of her energies into a healthy pregnancy, taking classes and researching and preparing for her next phase of life—motherhood. As she fretted over child care, baby feeding, and strollers, I started to understand why even though I may not have truly wanted a fourth child, I still wished for a pregnancy.

Wished for a pregnancy?! How could that be? Who likes pregnancy? I was forced to admit that I liked certain aspects of pregnancy—the commitment, the focus, the sense of importance, and a feeling of fulfilling your mission.

So if I were going to give up this fourth child and give up the chance at pregnancy—how could I get the best of both worlds? How could I get

Unpregnant? How could I still be purposeful, committed, and focused and fulfill my mission without the actual pregnancy? What could possibly be more important than this fourth baby; what could possibly be deserving of all that time, energy, and commitment? The answer: Otherhood. My other life.

During that spring, instead of wrestling with my disappointment (and boring my family and friends by whining about that never-to-be fourth baby) I began to enumerate what I would be postponing in *my* life if I did bring this child into the world. In that moment, I felt a steely resolve as I moved toward my idea of Unpregnancy.

One day I was sick about the baby I was never going to have and the family I would never round out to its intended potential and the next day, *Poof!* I was Unpregnant. I was on to new and different adventures. There was no turning back.

<hr>

Unpregnancy Is Nine Months for You

Unpregnancy is about what you want, what you remember wishing for, who you once thought you might become. Unpregnancy helps us all reclaim the positives of pregnancy and reapply them in our lives, now. Unpregnancy uses what every mother knows to help her get what every mother wants: Otherhood.

Unpregnancy is a strategy to change your life. Using the superpowers of pregnancy—the nine lessons learned in pregnancy—we can all get our dreams to come true in the context of our real lives.

If you're reading this, you have a real life and a family who's going to continue to need you and think of you as Mom. My family is my blessing and joy and I love to come home to them. I live to make their worlds exciting and interesting and I strive to push us all to live our best lives. My children have rich and wonderful lives: they take art lessons, join debate teams, try out for school musicals and play sports. But somewhere along the way, I realized that I was making their lives my whole life, and my life is too short for that. In fact, my life was coming up short. I needed Unpregnancy.

One Giant Leap for Mom-kind

As I've come to see, many, many other mothers needed Unpregnancy too. They needed to reconcile motherhood with ambition and to honor a vision or a calling that they could barely hear over the TV or the kids' squabbling. And they needed to see a new glimmer of a possibility without guilt or hopelessness. They needed a room of one's own, a chance to work, or the right to quit working. They needed to get out of the chauffeuring business and take the steering wheel of their own lives.

Through my seminars I've helped these mothers see the lessons of pregnancy and how to apply them in their current lives using *Motherhood to Otherhood* and helped them fashion their own Unpregnancies and make their lives over in a way that helped them feel happy and fulfilled. Most of them surprised themselves. What surprised me is how much pleasure I took in having a ringside seat at all of these extraordinary moments in great women's lives.

Over the years, I can remember a number of achievements that mothers happily attribute to coming to an Unpregnancy seminar and beginning to see their lives anew. I hope this book will extend that experience to a broad group of mothers equally interested in tapping into what every mother knows.

I'll share some of their successes here in order to give you an idea of the power of this concept and help you realize what each of us has inside once we breathe life into our dreams. These stories come from my seminar group experiences.

At one seminar session, a mother, Kristen told the group that she had no goals. Raising happy children was "extremely important to her," she told us, "and fulfilling." It was to remain her primary focus and her unpregnancy goal. She got a chorus of "no's" from the other moms. She could raise happy children and still pursue a goal for herself, they insisted. She admitted missing creative work, since she'd left behind a career in jewelry design. She absolutely didn't want to go back to jewelry design because it was too demanding—and so she was out of ideas. She liked knitting and used it as a creative outlet. By the time of her third trimester, she was busy planning a yarn store with a friend from her knitting group. Both the store and the yarn are gorgeous and they showcase Kristen's great talent and designer's eye.

Simone came to a seminar out of pure frustration, with no real plan. She had decided that she wanted to take her business solo, because her frequent disagreements with her partner were dragging her down. Her business was local, so out of fairness to the partner, she could not share her goal with the group. Nonetheless she said that the weekly meetings gave her a safe forum to give voice to her feelings, which grimly showed how little confidence remained between her and the partner. The seminars helped her define the necessary next steps to her own fulfillment.

Luz, an optimistic, positive mother, was ready to make time for herself. She and her five kids, including twins, had been displaced by a house fire. Her house was gutted and the rebuilding had dragged on for two years. Because the fire had kept them in hotels and rented houses, all five of her kids (ranging in age from 6 to 14) had their own cell phones. She was very connected: the children called her after school, practices, playdates or from home if she went out and she responded. "I'll be there soon. Look in the top drawer under the pencils. I didn't do laundry yet, wear the other one. Why didn't you tell me yesterday when we were at the store?" If five kids and a husband are each calling you a few times a day between 3:00 p.m. and 7:00 p.m., that's one call every 10 to 13 minutes. Luz needed Unpregnancy. Up until that point she resented the arduous and draining work of just getting her house back. She decided her goal would have be to embrace the work, make it creative and exciting, and get it done. Nothing else could proceed in her life until her family was resettled and less dependent on her.

Annabelle, a Girl Scout leader and social worker for high school kids, came to a seminar soon after her seven-year battle with Lyme disease. Once she was finally parasite-free and her energy returned, she struggled to define what was most important to her. She was trying to reorganize her house after years of neglect and still trying to decide whether to adopt a second child. She felt like she should reenter the workforce, but she was not sure if she wanted to. She is now back in a full-time job and is building a platform for the kind of speaking and research work she'd like to be able to transition to. For her, writing the Unpregnancy mission statement in Lesson #2 was an eye opener. Annabelle was a professional dancer before she got sick and had earned a Master's degree in social work. She had begun to combine the two passions in a program using art and dance as therapy. It was exciting and effective work that Annabelle felt passionate about. At a seminar, when the room full of moms read out their mission statements, she realized how unique hers was. She felt a drive to really dig into her profession and build art therapy as her specialty. She said, "I realized that if I didn't do it, who else would?"

Jo Ann worked as a speech pathologist. During a session at one of the seminar groups, she suddenly gasped. She said that she had just remembered a repressed goal: she had meant to get her PhD in speech pathology and had put it off when she got pregnant with her third child, who by now was nine years old. Until that moment, she hadn't noticed how long she had been drifting, not even thinking about her goals.

Christine didn't speak much at the seminar group she attended. She held a math and economics degree and an MBA. She still owed on her student loans, so she was not willing to contemplate going back to school for any training or degrees. She didn't want full-time work at a big corporation, where MBAs usually find gainful employment. About a week later, a national association of homeless shelters for families asked her to come to work for them. The hours were flexible, so when the opportunity arose, she jumped at it. A week earlier it wouldn't have occurred to her, but her Unpregnancy clarified her goals, and now she's glad to get momentum back in her life. "I'm paying off my loans. I'm doing something I feel good about and it's a good way for me to start thinking for the long term. I love, love my job," says Christine.

Tracy's 10-year-old son was born with a rare genetic disorder and he had had several near-death emergencies and surgeries in his short life. Tracy's life and options were circumscribed by the time and schedule required to care for him adequately. Yet Tracy was calm, smiling, and very positive. Through her Unpregnancy, Tracy created a nonprofit organization to distribute a video she produced about her son's disease. She also began to work with families whose lives had been touched by the disease and to create an international advocacy group. She brought her new video for us all to see and we were impressed by the upbeat, informative, hopeful message it conveyed. Her foundation now sells the video to families and hospitals and teaching centers around the world.

Linda says Unpregnancy really helped her value her personal goals. She is a cellist who had given up trying to play years earlier. Because of her

Unpregnancy, she prioritized playing and said later: "I've grown with my music [and] I'm even teaching. Now that I've joined a quartet and a symphony orchestra, my kids see a side of me that makes them so proud of their mommy. Mommy is more than Mommy now. She's a professional musician."

Jessica had an unusual goal. In fact, it made no sense to most of us when she first said that what she really wanted was to trade in her minivan for a red convertible. I was sure she meant it symbolically, but a few weeks later, Jessica drove up in her new red sports car! It was a beautiful day and Jessica looked 10 years younger. I chided her that it was usually men who bought sports cars in their midlife crises. She replied, "It's something I always wanted and never felt I deserved. We had two minivans and we'd outgrown car seats. A red convertible just popped into my head as something I could have if I wanted it. I love it. The other day after working on a Saturday, I came out in the parking lot and there it was, my little sports car. I felt like it was greeting me. I felt like it was my boyfriend surprising me after a late shift at work and I was a teenager again."

❧ ⬦ ☙

Unpregnancy is by, for, and about you. Your goals and dreams are so widely varied, interesting and exciting. These women were bogged down—happy mothers, but unfulfilled women—who hoped to reconnect with *Motherhood to Otherhood* to satisfy an itch, undo an ache and fulfill a wish.

Unpregnancy reclaims what you and all mothers know. What you learned during pregnancy could fill a book.

JOURNAL ENTRY

I was trying to get Unpregnant.

My urgent desire to be Unpregnant isn't a shameful secret. I did not throw myself down the stairs or try a Coke douche on prom night.

I am Unpregnant and proud of it.

I'm 40. My husband and I have our three children, ages nine, six, and three, and they are unique and wonderful humans. Each is an extraordinary addition to the world. We have offbeat, brilliant, and funny children whose future (and future impact on a future world) I cannot predict.

I long for the commitment of pregnancy. When you're pregnant, you commit. You don't hedge, wait, consider, or bargain, you just commit. It's a done deal. Nine months from now, you're going to have a baby.

And there are certain inevitabilities:

Your body is going to change and sometimes feel like something alien.

You quit drinking (or smoking, if that's your vice).

You eat well; you drink milk.

You get your rest.

You take good care of yourself.

People you hardly know touch your belly.

People get excited and talk about your body.

You feel good about your body—most days.

You feel depressed about your body—most days.

Pregnancy is a very positive and exciting time and it's a learning experience.

I learned to respect and admire my body and to view it for more than its shape or size.

I ate for positive reasons. My body needed fuel, the right fuel. I exercised to maintain my energy and keep my back from aching. My tolerance for fat, white wine, smoke, and even salty food became very low. I could actually feel how those things hurt my body.

I got heartburn, I was so thirsty I couldn't sleep and I had an acute aversion to smoke, even outdoors.

I would never have risked taboo behavior with a small wonder in my womb. I was committed and positive; there were no recriminations, dread or feelings of deprivation. I was nourishing one of my children. And I was nourishing me. I was really eating for two. Psychologically, I had earned the right to nourishment and nurturing from myself. And when I faltered in that right or erred toward chocolate ice cream, I had a nautical newborn on-board helping to keep me on an even keel. I want my rebirth. Forty weeks from now I want to give birth to the newborn who is me, the newborn who will take on my new life with the curiosity, excitement and energy that you can only achieve from a true sense of enthusiasm.

I feel that my forty-week Unpregnancy is my time. I have no distinct plans. I want to find out what I want—and not a boy or girl. What I want for me. It is my first Unpregnancy, so I don't know what to expect.

*I hope to feel as valued and important as I did with my first pregnancy.
I hope to feel as excited and blissful as I was when I was growing my first child
and changing my life forever. I hope to feel fear mingled with awe. I hope to worry
about whether I'll be good enough, whether I can do it, whether I can succeed in
my new life. I hope to truly grow and give birth to something I cannot conceive
of right now and whose future—and future impact on the world—I cannot
predict. Some new me.*

*For nine months, I will be obsessed and moody and I will need extra sleep.
I will refuse certain invitations. I will indulge cravings. I will deserve whatever
I identify as my desire. I will be the fickle, fabled, finicky female known as
The Unpregnant.*

* *I will feed my body and lose weight.*
* *I will feed my soul and lose everyday clutter.*
* *I will feed my marriage and regain the joy and pleasure of my husband's
  company and support.*
* *I will feed my creativity and ideas with the same awe, delight, support and
  indulgence that I usually reserve for my children and their ideas.*
* *I will feed my belief in myself and my future.*

With these vows neatly inscribed in my journal, I knew I was committed
to Otherhood—changing my life and getting something from this Unpregnancy. Still, I had a long way to go. I was excited, but clueless. It was the same
feeling I had had years before when leaving my obstetrician's office with the
first indication that I was headed into unknown territory. I mean *big* unknown
territory.

how to use this book

It should be clear by now that *Motherhood to Otherhood* is not a parenting book. As I'm sure you know, there are scores of books on how to be a good mother to your children. This is a book about how to be a good mother to yourself, how to raise your Self to be the best person you can be by using all your experiences as a mother.

As mothers we have an undermined, undervalued gift in our lives—pregnancy and birth. These experiences taught us all so much about how to live great lives. But raising children can be so all-consuming that we rarely think back to pregnancy. We can hardly remember a time when we didn't have kids or who we once hoped to be. Now, when we think ahead, it is naturally about our kids' futures. Sometimes we wish for things for ourselves, but we feel we cannot—or should not—even try for them because of our kids' pre-emptive needs. Even if you have a full-time job, you have another job at home, so prioritizing your own needs can be sidetracked, sometimes for decades.

Motherhood to Otherhood is a new model for how to succeed, for how to get the life *you really want,* using the *lessons you've already learned*. Pregnancy was a time of great commitment, urgency, excitement and focus. You have the motivational model in your own life for how to change everything in nine months and come away happy, even blissful.

In this section, I've outlined the book by explaining what to expect when you're (un)expecting. Since I am recommending that you spend nine months on your Unpregnancy, I'd like to explain how the book and other Unpregnancy tools (like the website www.unpregnancy.com) can be woven in and out of your Unpregnancy undertaking.

Three Trimesters to Change

The Unpregnancy plan is set up in three trimesters to address the three major areas of anyone's life:

T1/**SELF**—self-improvement goals

T2/**LOVE**—strengthening relationships with friends or family

T3/**WORK**—finding and pursuing your life's work

It's best to conceive and pursue the goals in that order and time frame. First, you choose a self-oriented goal, like quitting smoking or losing weight or training for a marathon or whatever you feel holds you back from pursuing larger life goals. You begin that goal in earnest for the first three months until you're ready to add in a family-oriented goal.

In the second trimester, you continue supporting your first goal and you add in a second goal. Your primary focus will shift to the family or friendship-related goal, like repairing a relationship or empowering a family member to succeed or getting the love you want. Finally, after six months, with heart and home well supported, you are ready to layer in your work goal, whether it's in community or career.

Each trimester's focus is important and each goal achievement makes an enormous contribution to your newly changed life. If you can, decide on all three goals in the beginning of the Unpregnancy, so you can support success in all three areas during your whole Unpregnancy. This gives you time to get used to the long-term expectations and make the changes you'll need in your life to usher in the new era.

Nine Lessons

❋ Each trimester has three lessons (for a total of nine), which remind us of a lesson learned in pregnancy and reapplies that lesson to our everyday lives now.

❋ The lessons are self-evident, although the ways in which they apply to your life now will not be.

LESSON #1: You'll Never Be Alone Again

LESSON #2: Only You Can Do This

LESSON #3: You Are Great, with Child

LESSON #4: You're Gestating (Everything Else Can Wait)

LESSON #5: You Don't Know What to Expect

LESSON #6: Napping Is Not a Crime

LESSON #7: Is Mother Nature Kidding Me?

LESSON #8: Keep Your Eyes on the Prize

LESSON #9: Nothing Can Stop You in the Homestretch

Forty Labors

❋ Each lesson has 4 to 6 "labors" (for a total of 40). A "labor" is an exercise that can help you identify your goal or help you move your project along.

❋ Take your time with the labors. They are self-revealing and often fun!

❋ Some work better with input from others, so do them with friends, other Unpregnant women, or online at www.unpregnancy.com along with the virtual community of mothers.

Checkups

❋ Of course there are checkups. You need to be honest with yourself about progress in each trimester.

❋ In the last chapter you'll find the mother of all checkups, which recaps the nine lessons and gives you space to write in your thoughts and reactions to the lesson.

Getting Started

Begin at the beginning, with enthusiasm. Once you've committed yourself to the three goals at the end of this introduction, you can proceed as best suits you. How you use the readings and labors to support your Unpregnancy and what kind of community you create for yourself is determined by who you are naturally and how you approached pregnancy in the first place. Some people research and prepare, others like to dive in head first.

I've hosted women from all walks of life in small Unpregnancy groups all around the country. Some met for two days, learning all the lessons up front and then going on to apply them to their lives. Others met weekly for nine weeks to learn and absorb a lesson per week. Both groups of women tended to bond deeply with each other and continue to meet without me for the remainder of their Unpregnancies. Time and time again, I'm told that the biggest reason that these mothers had a great experience with their Unpregnancies is the sustenance provided by their group of mothers.

The groups that met for two days did an overview of the lessons first and then went back month by month repeating the lessons, going into more depth as each lesson occurred chronologically in their Unpregnancies. The groups who met for nine weeks had given each lesson an in-depth look by their seminar's end and had launched a fully informed Unpregnancy. While both methods were effective, I think the lesson per week fits into most people's lives well, creates a good pace and focus, and is the best way to use this book.

Read one lesson per week.

First, read the introduction and decide on your goals. As you enter the first trimester and begin work on your Self Goal, continue reading the lessons and doing the self-exploration labors. A steady rate of one lesson per week is productive. By the time you're nine weeks into your first trimester, you're centered, committed, and empowered by everything you learned during pregnancy. You will have made significant progress in your first trimester and will be primed for your own fruitful Unpregnancy.

It isn't advisable to do only one lesson per month or one labor per week because you will be taking in the information too slowly to effect grand change in the nine-month time frame. If you pursue the book at this pace, you may find that the Unpregnancy plan won't have a full or lasting impact on a mother's busy life.

Return to the book periodically for support and inspiration.

Months into the plan, when you're entering a new trimester, dip back in for a refresher course. When there's a lesson that comes into play in your life, you can reread those few pages for guidance, inspiration, and validation.

Make a specific commitment to return to the book for your checkup every trimester. The checkup will help you recall the lessons and lead you back to any labors you may have skipped earlier. Later in your Unpregnancy, you may have more time and a slightly different perspective to do the labors.

Visit www.unpregnancy.com for free e-tools.

I strongly recommend that you stay connected to Unpregnancy and make it work for you for the entire term. www.unpregnancy.com offers an online community of mothers sharing experiences, making recommendations about how to achieve goals, and sharing the frustrations and triumphs of Unpregnancy. Much of the content is user-generated by great moms like yourself—so visit for guidance and stay to give your advice and ideas. Mother yourself and others! Join the online community of Unpregnant women striving to live their best lives.

Form your own Unpregnancy group.

Great change comes from dramatic change in perspective and expectations. To get a fresh look at your life, create your own Unpregnancy group. Get together in a community center, at a coffee house, or in someone's home. You can rotate who will host. If there is a group of you with small children, get a group sitter for the meeting so you can talk uninterrupted. For best results have the child dropoff at a separate house from your Unpregnancy meeting. Consider meeting in a room at a library. The librarian can even refer you to books and trade magazines that will support your individual efforts. She might also be willing to help you promote a *Motherhood to Otherhood* group by posting signs in the library. How about timing the group meeting to coincide with a toddler story hour?

Each week, you can discuss the lessons in a chapter, progress made in your pursuit of your goals and milestones achieved. Just give everyone a 10-minute chance to talk. My experience is that if you begin with anywhere from 6 to 10 mothers, you will always have enough people to meet each week and your group will be sustained even if someone drops out or someone gets sick. You can meet weekly or bi-weekly for the first nine weeks to discuss the nine lessons of Unpregnancy and then continue to get together monthly for the entire nine months.

You will be amazed what a group of women can do for each other, even if their goals are different from one another's. You share a commonality that comes from changing expectations, struggling with defining a mission, overcoming obstacles, and celebrating successes. Where but among like-minded friends can you trust and bond enough to grow and change? You need a forum for your hopes, fears, and frustrations. We can't keep it all bottled up when we're facing scary propositions.

Among friends, you can share an easy laugh at your own expense. During one meeting Kathy rushed in late. She struggled to take off her jacket quickly when her water bottle dropped to the ground. *Look everyone, Kathy's water broke,* I said. We laughed till we had tears in our eyes. Maybe you had to be there, but that's precisely the point. Be there for each other.

Find a midwife.

A midwife is someone who helps you during pregnancy and birth. If you cannot find or organize a group, find a second woman to share your Unpregnancy experience with. If you know a great mom whom you'd like to share this experience with, get her a copy of the book. Give it to her and let her catch up. She might live near you so you can get together regularly or you two might work virtually. If you're looking for a midwife, go to www.unpregnancy.com and post a request for a midwife.

If you're in an Unpregnancy group, establish midwives.

Place everyone's name in a "midwife" container and let each choose another's name. As someone's midwife, you are responsible for sending your Unpregnant friend notes about herself on a regular basis. They can be anything complimentary, such as:

- **I admire your stance in life.**
- **I can see by the changes in your wardrobe that you have a new lease on life.**
- **Thank you for sharing your experiences—it helped a lot of us.**

Midwife notes should be specific, positive and anonymous. To deliver your note, simply mark it with your recipient's name and place it back in the container. At the end of each meeting, the notes can be handed out to the appropriate recipients. Midwife notes have a tremendously powerful impact on your spirit. We are all struggling with a goal (or three), trying out our new selves, and we aren't accustomed to being noticed or getting compliments. You will be receiving notes from your midwife, so you'll know how they radiate positive energy and how they can make you smile or put a spring in your step.

Though you have a responsibility to make sure your designated recipient gets notes and feedback from you, you are encouraged to send anonymous notes to anyone in your group. The more positive feedback, the better.

a cure for
morning sickness

Pregnancy wakes you up to that queasy, uneasy feeling, resulting in a grab for the nearest receptacle. Unpregnancy—with everything you're striving for—may provide the same sort of awakening, unfortunately. At least with Unpregnancy we're talking in metaphors. The best receptacle for your unease during Unpregnancy is a Morning Journal.

I am grateful to Julia Cameron's *Artists' Way* for this life-affirming daily habit. Just write—don't think, don't edit, just let your pen move along over two or three pages in a journal every morning. This is your Morning Journal, where you can finally hear and respond to your inner voice. This is where you can *get it out*. What *you* think is all that matters. And what you think can find an audience, an advocate, an ally, and an action plan.

As Cameron says, "Morning pages do get us to the other side: the other side of our own fear, of our negativity, of our minds." Could all this really happen just because you wrote a couple of pages each morning? Like prenatal vitamins, I consider a Morning Journal to be vital to all Unpregnancies. I am a stalwart advocate for such writing because it has been the single strongest agent for change in my life.

I know there is strong resistance out there. People resist writing because they don't feel they have time, or they worry that they can't even write well enough to keep a journal and will feel as if they're putting on airs. Or they just find it intimidating to write what they're thinking. Some want to write, but feel it is selfish when there is so much else to do.

Many moms confide that they're afraid their husbands or kids will read what they write or be suspicious about why Mom is writing all the time. Lock it up or let it be read—it's your choice. My own journal is so boringly focused on me that no one seems to care to read it. If they've dipped in out of curiosity, two paragraphs was all they could take before they fell into a deep slumber. Or if you're concerned about long-term privacy, write on regular loose leaf paper that you can throw away at the end of each week. But at least allow yourself to see and hear your thoughts and ideas.

If you're feeling self-conscious, that's wonderful. This program is intended to be consciousness-raising. Get to know yourself.

I can hear many of you groaning about the time commitment. You can fit it in! Who had time for morning sickness? Who welcomed that symptom? But imagine keeping it in, ignoring the toxic buildup and not letting it out. Negativity and fear can jam us up. If you don't write every day, so what? If it's not first thing in the morning, fine. Let your journal be part of your morning routine most days and you'll feel the results. Some people prefer to write at night. If you drop it for months at a time, then just pick it back up when you need it, so you can think on paper.

Yes, it's true, many of us think writing is b-o-o-o-oring. Talk about bringing out your inner child, your moping, sulking, foot-dragging child. It might be a little boring. Are you boring? Sometimes. My own journal is pure drivel, just my daily thoughts, rarely even re-readable. But writing down my thoughts helps me separate what is actually drivel from what is important to me. It keeps me from boring my friends to death with the same litany of complaints and petty fears.

This is your chance to hear your inner voice and respond to your stated needs. This is your inner baby crying on the page, delighting in a minor accomplishment, indulging in a little fantasy. If you write two to three pages a day in a journal, you will get to know yourself in a new way. These aren't meant to be literate, reusable, valuable pages, just whatever comes to mind that morning—unedited self-expression, written and reread without judging yourself. If you put your concern down on paper daily, you can dismiss it and feel better or realize you can't dismiss it and you need to do something about it. You can see what's making you happy, sad, angry, or stressed.

Unpregnancy provides context. Using your Unpregnancy experience like a pregnancy gives you a frame of reference from your own life. Pregnancy was a time of great discomfort, pain, fear, yet excitement, purpose, awe, wonder and power. Exploring those same elements in a journal during your Unpregnancy can help you bring about great change in your life. So despite your objections, try writing every day or most days for at least your first trimester. Let yourself out to play.

three trimesters
to change

To achieve the biggest effect in nine months, I knew I had to do more than go on *another* diet or get a new hobby. I knew I had to map out a full-scale life change. If I was going to give up a real, breathing fourth child, I had to give myself back something big to fill that void. I needed to contribute to my soul with new ideas, experiences and opportunities. Just as a child brings you curious eyes and a fresh point of view, I was looking forward to a new vision: my own.

My pregnancies had had a purpose with a strong pulse, a life force. My single-minded pregnancy mission was to stay healthy and happy and to get ready for the baby growing inside me. For Unpregnancy to have that same life force and unswerving purpose, I knew I had to imbue it with a mission which was undeniably important and wondrous to me.

How could my Unpregnancy be that huge, that undeniable, that much of a force in my life—my whole life? How could it knock me down and pick me back up again, just as pregnancy and birth had? I had to find my way back to what every mother knows, what I'd taken away from my experiences of pregnancy and birth.

I worked to give my Unpregnancy the magnitude of a true pregnancy. As it took shape in my mind, I realized it would have to have three trimesters, thereby giving it the natural progression from a private, personal "condition" to one that eventually became obvious even to strangers. As much as possible, I wanted this Unpregnancy to deliver me into the world a changed woman—somehow new and yet still me. I wanted it to get me to Otherhood.

The first step was to ensure that my goals were meaningful to me—*vital to me*—and to make sure that they addressed my whole life. Second, if the goals were to be enormous, life-altering, then you'd need time (like nine months, maybe?) to adjust your thinking, figure out how to get there, and acclimate the people around you to the changes and new expectations. Thirdly, Unpregnancy growth would need to proceed much like a pregnancy: the first trimester is just for you; in the second, you share your news (and goals) with your family and friends. During your third trimester you're so big, the world knows. You have a different glow about you and you're getting ready to assume your new job as a mother.

Each Unpregnancy trimester prioritizes a different set of goals. What you choose to undertake, trimester by trimester, must be part of a grand life plan that excites you (with nine months of concerted effort and focus, you can get there).

Three Trimesters of Unpregnancy: Self—Love—Work

The idea of three trimesters came to me organically. Like a pregnant belly, like a baby growing inside you, it made sense to me to reconstruct my life from the inside out. My own needs came first, family second, and then I'd be ready to make the right work choices and goals. You have to start with your own needs before you can become the person you dream of becoming. It's the same premise as the in-flight instructions during an emergency—they tell you to put on your own oxygen mask first. Help yourself before you help your child. You have to remain alert in order to help the child. (Maybe it seems selfish, but it's essential.)

In researching *Motherhood to Otherhood,* I came across *The Hierarchy of Human Needs,* developed by Dr. Abraham Maslow, which supports this me-first point of view. Maslow's theory is that people have a deep desire to self-actualize, but must meet imperative needs first. Maslow describes self-actualization as:

> *"A musician must make music, an artist must paint, a poet must write . . . to be at peace . . . . This is the need we call self-actualization. . . . It refers to [the] desire for fulfillment, namely to the tendency to become actually what one is potentially: to become everything that one is capable of becoming . . ."*

Maslow says there are two processes necessary for self-actualization: self-exploration and action. Unpregnancy gives you ample opportunity for both. You can find your unmet needs and address them in each of three life areas: Self-Love-Work. You can evolve as you meet basic needs and begin work on higher need levels to help you self-actualize.

MASLOW'S HIERARCHY OF HUMAN NEEDS

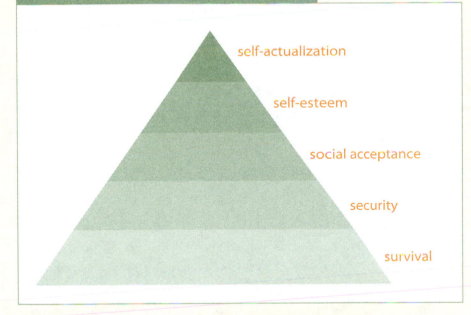

self-actualization

self-esteem

social acceptance

security

survival

Humans naturally strive for growth and love. Unfulfilled needs create anxiety, frustration, anger, and resentment. (As the saying goes, resentment is the poison *we* take to punish *them*.) Your needs could be at any level of the pyramid, from obvious and identifiable needs such as food, shelter, and air, to more nebulous needs at higher levels, like the need to paint, manage property, or become politically involved. We may simply need recognition for what we are doing, so we can get satisfaction and strive to do more. Higher-level needs are harder to pinpoint and so it is harder to diagnose what you might need to feel happier, more at peace. In addition, higher-level needs might seem more selfish, particularly when you're aware of others who are needier.

It is important to realize the value of your unmet needs and to understand that it is a justifiable use of your time to address them. Acknowledge the fact that you have to start where you are, meeting your own needs first.

In your first trimester (T1), you begin with your Self—your health, your spirit, your energy, your self-expression. In your second trimester (T2), you address your Love—family relationships, friendships. In your third trimester (T3), you begin to tackle your life's Work: a career, a community role, a creative undertaking.

For some mothers, the goals have happened sequentially, neatly beginning on schedule as they enter the appropriate trimester. For others all three goals are present and pressing throughout their nine months. If you are driven to begin all three trimester goals from day one, you should at least acknowledge each trimester's *priority*. If push comes to shove in the first trimester, your self–focused goals prevail (meet your most basic needs first). Do not deprive yourself and press forward. Not yet. Promise yourself you'll protect yourself and your self-directed goals as a priority during the first trimester, your love and your love goals as a priority during your second trimester, and your work and your work goals as a priority during your third and last trimester.

Goals will overlap by necessity. Your first trimester goals will extend for the entire nine months just as you maintained your health as a priority throughout your real pregnancy. When you're ready to begin family goals, you'll continue to support the personal growth and endeavors you started in your first trimester. As third trimester goals take you outside the home, that doesn't mean you'll abandon the achievements of your first two trimesters. You'll continue to support your successes and strive to achieve more on all three goal sets. You must continue to protect and nurture the growth you've achieved in prior trimesters.

By the end of your Unpregnancy, you will have revamped three major areas of your daily life—yourself, your family relations, and your community or career options. You will have changed the way people see you and react to you.

You will have birthed a new and exciting (and fulfilled) you.

conception

This is the fun part, right? Now you get to decide who you want to be and how to get there. This is an exciting moment, full of possibilities. It is forbidden fruit or forgotten lust, a fantasy come to life. This is your chance to really speak from your heart and get what you desire. Desire can be exhilarating when fulfilled, but devastating when repressed or unrequited. Let your desires bubble up and face your dreams. Don't worry about how your desire tumbles out right now: it doesn't need to be orderly; it does not need to be realistic or reasonable. Take your time. Indulge yourself.

To consider what you really want, try one or more of these brainstorming methods. They are roughly grouped according to trimester, but try whatever you think will help you conceive the new you. You can also visit www.unpregnancy.com to see what other mothers are doing and how it makes them feel!

* **Self**
    * Take a long walk in a park or hike along a path. Slip a paper and pen in your pocket so you can write down ideas when they're fresh and exciting.
    * Take a bubble bath, using candles and scents to relax, and let the world slip away. Make sure you use this relaxing time to get in touch with your inner self, your untapped desires, your scary aspirations.
    * Work out. Don't use TV or reading to distract you. Let your mind focus first on the bodily effort and then once you get going, let your mind wander and great ideas will form.
    * Run away from home! Take an evening out, a weekend away, or half an hour at a coffeehouse. Take what you need.
    * Think of bad habits, compulsions, and addictions that you're ready to face. Imagine how ridding yourself of such habits will help you and everyone around you.
    * Get a massage.

❋ **Love**

- Consider relationships that are more of a struggle than they used to be.
- Ask yourself, *am I getting the love I want?*
- Take a weekend with girlfriends and just talk.
- Try a full day of just listening. Try not to talk at all, if you can. By listening and not talking, you might hear a completely different family.
- Think of things that would greatly improve your life and your respect for yourself and from others.

❋ **Work**

- Consider whom you're jealous of—what does she have that you wish you had? How does she manage it? How could you? What are the steps? What would you do differently from her? Could you talk to her and ask her how she achieved her position, attitude, freedom?
- Consider activities that you loved as a girl or young woman.
- Consider dreams you had for your life. Were you hoping to be a writer? A politician? A dancer? Did you consider yourself a pretty good sculptor? Are you an excellent cook or baker?
- Talk and listen. Call old friends or your sisters and your mother to reminisce about your girlish dreams and expectations. They can be the path back to what you want now.
- Take a day off in a city to wander and ponder what you truly want. Go to an art museum, ice skating, or bowling.
- Flip through women's magazines. Could you see yourself in the roles portrayed? As a model? As a designer? As a CEO? Cop? Advertising exec? Entrepreneur? Chef? Nurse? What gets your attention and your admiration?

Where will your Unpregnancy take you? Jot down some initial ideas of what you wish for. Your goals may come three at a time, like rungs on a ladder, or you may need three different brainstorming episodes to decide on your course.

If you have more than one idea per trimester, don't worry, you can narrow it down later:

Self

_____

_____

_____

_____

_____

_____

Love

_____

_____

_____

_____

_____

_____

Work

_____

_____

_____

_____

_____

_____

Your three goals may be interconnected or may be individual yet vital accomplishments. If you find one inspiring, imperative goal per trimester, you will undoubtedly build toward the life you want, even if the goals seem unrelated right now. You will connect the dots later. If it's really important to you, go for it. Once you've achieved it, you'll be able to see why you needed to do that.

In my own experience, my goals appeared unrelated but added up to who I wanted to be. I wanted to lose weight. (It was weighing me down.) It didn't seem like a truly worthy goal to me and it wasn't anything I could get excited about. But as a life example to my young kids about taking responsibility for your health and as the first step toward becoming a writer (and possibly a guest on a talk show), losing weight became essential. My three goals added up to a life I am proud of and excited to live. In the context of my other two goals, I could finally see it was something I had to undertake to get where I wanted in my whole life. I needed to get it behind me to free up my time and focus for other endeavors; and I needed to be slimmer to achieve my Work goals. I was finally able to embrace diet and exercise and lose 50 pounds in my first Unpregnancy. I could see the purpose and ultimate reward—i.e., why it was worth the self-sacrifice and focus in the context of my whole Unpregnancy plan. And I was able through Unpregnancy to approach weight-loss with self-caring instead of self-deprivation for the first time in my life. Unpregnancy gave me the mission, the nurturing, and the positive outlook to commit to and achieve this lifelong, elusive goal.

In my first Unpregnancy, I lost weight and gained health and energy. I worked with each of my three kids to design and decorate new rooms for them. My husband and I shared an empowering marriage seminar and reconnected lovingly. Later in the year we took a romantic cruise together. I committed to friends and neighbors to get our community a public pool. I developed the concept of Unpregnancy, lived by it, and kept a journal. I also attended a weekend career seminar where I told 75 women about Unpregnancy for the very first time.

In my second Unpregnancy, I continued to seek health and fitness by continuing and increasing my workout routines. I quit drinking alcohol and I powered my new life with calm, pleasant energy. I took my kids on a cross-country RV trip, after which we wrote a great book together, entitled *RV There Yet?* They got to see what happens when you keep a journal, craft it into a published work, and put your creativity out into the world. In my third trimester, I assembled my first-ever Unpregnancy seminar, hosted a group of women weekly, and began writing *Motherhood to Otherhood.*

Unpregnancy began to take on a life of its own and I knew I had to share it with all Mom-kind.

Choosing Goals

Go for broke! Have you ever heard of anyone being a little pregnant? Can you imagine beginning a pregnancy hoping for a little bit more baby? No! You want a whole baby—the whole enchilada. This is your Unpregnancy. Once you figure out what you really want, then go for it. In nine months you'll have changed your life forever. And like a baby, once your goals are launched, they will grow and take on a life of their own and shape your world forever.

We sometimes refer to a creation as a brainchild or refer to a project as "my baby." Clearly, there is an intuitive connection. If you find your goals are central to your life, your Unpregnancy will become as important to you as your real children and your new endeavors will grow and bring you new friends, new experiences, even a new vocabulary. (Can't you remember a time when you didn't know what a layette was? Or why anyone would need a diaper wipes warmer?)

Look back at the list of ideas you had above. Any or all of these goals may feature in your Unpregnancy. Just as you may have "dabbled" premaritally, you have time to dabble now. The key is to avoid becoming Unpregnant with the wrong dalliance: find your calling, not just a way to fill time.

This is the time to give all your ideas consideration, to believe that there's no such thing as a bad idea. You may not pursue your wildest idea, but you want to let it bubble up and be given fair play. Sometimes a crazy idea gives you insight into what you actually want. Let yourself linger here and contemplate what you're going to devote yourself to for the next nine months. The strength of the goal, its appeal, and its necessity in your life form the basis for a strong and effective Unpregnancy. Begin your Unpregnancy when you are ready to commit and devote yourself to a new you.

Goal Ideas

There are as many dreams and goals as there are people to embrace them. Here's a short list to get you started.

T1/SELF

- Find a room of your own
- Get more sleep
- Lose weight
- Don't diet—embrace your body
- Quit smoking
- Get fit
- Quit drinking alcohol
- Dress better
- Relax more often
- Lower your cholesterol or blood pressure
- Manage your health better
- Develop your gratitude
- Get therapy
- Consider plastic surgery
- Enjoy each moment
- Live without fear
- Take on a new sport
- Indulge a creative muse
- Keep a creative journal
- Build your vocabulary
- Do something you've always been afraid to try
- Write/paint/create
- Begin yoga or Pilates
- Take up horseback riding
- Try stand-up comedy or acting

T2/LOVE

- Go out with friends more
- Create a weekly date night with your husband
- Have a long-distance phone night each month
- Spend time alone with each kid
- Address issues with parents, siblings, or in-laws
- Get marriage counseling with your husband
- Greet your family members enthusiastically each day
- Teach your kids a skill/craft you want to share
- Create a playroom or craft room
- Decorate or renovate rooms with the kids' input
- Seek a more satisfying sex life
- Say yes whenever you can, no when you can't

- Reconnect with teenage kids
- Repair an important relationship
- Seek romance after divorce
- Go cross-country with your family
- Learn to depend less on your husband or partner

T3/WORK

Career

- Reenter the workforce
- Do what you love to do
- Spend more of each day creatively
- Go freelance
- Start a company
- Raise hourly rates
- Begin a speaking career
- Earn a professional certificate or degree
- Get a raise/promotion
- Join a networking group
- Consult a life coach
- Investigate franchise opportunities
- Take a career seminar
- Write your memoirs
- Transition to a new career
- Develop artistic credibility

Community

- Try public speaking
- Take a seat on a not-for-profit board
- Get involved in your community
- Run for public office
- Found a not-for-profit org
- Take a job in your local community
- Volunteer for an integral role in your church or synagogue
- Make a difference in your town in a way that matters to you
- Join or run a local chapter of a fundraising group
- Volunteer at a homeless shelter or soup kitchen
- Develop or join a community improvement project
- Donate your professional skills—accounting, therapy, copywriting—to a not-for-profit effort

Your Unpregnancy Goals

When you're ready, write down what you want for yourself in the next nine months.

T1/Self

_____

_____

T2/Love

_____

_____

T3/Work

_____

_____

Don't worry if how you'll do these things is unclear at this time. Don't even worry if you only have a general idea about your second and third trimester goals right now. When you were growing a perfect life inside you, all you really worried about at first was ten fingers and ten toes. That's not a bad place to start. So just get started.

Testing Your Goals

Unpregnancy intends to turn dreams into goals and goals into change. None of this can come true for you unless your goals are _critical_ to you. You must spend time internalizing why the goals mean so much to you. You need to know that the Unpregnancy you're about to undertake will hold a central position of importance in your life throughout a nine-month period. The reward—the new you—needs to be something you can visualize, something you can achieve, and something you _want_.

The questions below will help you to decide whether each goal deserves a central position in your life over the term of your Unpregnancy.

If you achieved these goals, how would your life be different?

1. Self:

2. Love:

3. Work:

What would you feel if you didn't achieve these goals?

1. Self:

2. Love:

3. Work:

How would you react:

If someone said you could not pursue these goals? You're forbidden:

1. Self:

2. Love:

3. Work:

If someone told you, "You aren't good enough or smart enough to do this."

1. Self:

2. Love:

3. Work:

If someone said, "Don't waste your time."

1. Self:

2. Love:

3. Work:

Ask yourself:

Is this truly an important goal for me?

1. Self: _____

2. Love: _____

3. Work: _____

Am I pulling up short?

1. Self: _____

2. Love: _____

3. Work: _____

Am I ready to commit?

1. Self: _____

2. Love: _____

3. Work: _____

If not now, when?

1. Self: _____

2. Love: _____

3. Work: _____

You are the expert. You have the experience to draw on. Remember that, like pregnancy and birth, no great or significant change happens quickly or easily. But there is a powerful force for change deep inside you. . . . waiting to be born.

how to get unpregnant

You've chosen and tested your goals. You know why these goals are so important in your life. You know you have the experience of pregnancy to draw upon for a strong sense of commitment and purpose.

You feel awe mingled with fear. You're anxious to get going.

How do you get Unpregnant?

JOURNAL ENTRY

I was looking for a sign, a sign that I was Unpregnant. I wanted to get going. Quit overeating. Feel committed. Begin my nine-month odyssey.

I needed a sign. What could it be? I went to the dentist and he put the big heavy apron on me and took X-rays. I thought to myself, "Excuse me. I'm Unpregnant. I shouldn't be exposed to X-rays." Of course, he needed the X-rays for dental work. It sounded stupid, even to me. I guess I wasn't Unpregnant yet.

I was refinishing furniture. The oil-based polyurethane and varnish were definitely headachey. I worked in the garage and had good ventilation, but I would never have done that during a pregnancy. I refinished the furniture. Does that mean I'm not Unpregnant yet? Who knows? What are the rules of Unpregnancy? I didn't intend to act as if I were pregnant. At any rate, I didn't feel Unpregnant, committed

Then, strangely enough, I had a distinct sign. I thought I was pregnant. I really thought I was pregnant. Obviously, we weren't planning another child. That's what this Unpregnancy is about. I want to get beyond babies, bottles, and limited vision. I want to grow as my small children grow, into the broader world. I want to get BIG. So now I know how you get Unpregnant. You buy a pregnancy test. Any Tuesday will do. No need for signs. No need to delay. Buy a pregnancy test. Take it. Two lines, you're pregnant. One line, you're Unpregnant. Celebrate.

Here it is. Your nine months. Your Unpregnancy. Your way-past-postpartum odyssey to rebirth.

Congratulations, You're Unpregnant

You just found out you're Unpregnant.

The reality of it tingles up your spine and settles in your smile.

You're the first to know this powerful secret.

You have chosen to be Unpregnant, chosen to reclaim what you learned in pregnancy to grow something big and new in your life now.

It'll be a new life . . . yours.

This time, it's personal. You're not pregnant, you're Unpregnant.

You will dedicate the next nine months to nurturing yourself and your goals. You will relearn and reapply the nine self-evident lessons of pregnancy to help you reshape your life.

Reclaim your time, find your center, and share your newfound joy and ambition. In three trimesters you will revamp your Self, your Love relationships, and your life's Work.

Expect big changes in a relatively short time frame.

In just nine months, Unpregnancy can literally change your life.

And you know it can happen. You've seen it before.

Maybe you still can't believe the wonderful news. Maybe you still don't have a clear picture of how you'll achieve your rebirth. This is just the beginning. You're understandably a little stunned. Today is just the first day.

your unpregnancy	your goal		begin date	end date
T1/Self			(Today)	(+280 days)
T2/Love			(+94 days)	(+280 days)
T3/Work			(+186 days)	(+280 days)
Signed:			Date:	

Save this page! When you waver in your commitment, come back to this chart to remember why these goals were important to you. Visit www.unpregnancy.com for a due date calculator. You can enter today's date (or another start date) and map out your trimesters' start dates and plan toward your Unbirthday—280 days from now!

month	1	2	3	4	5	6	7	8	9
T1/Self									
T2/Love									
T3/Work									

PART ONE:

put yourself first

first trimester—self

Your Unpregnancy begins with you, naturally. Remember when you first found out you were pregnant? You were blissfully alone. Nothing else seemed significant. Other people's realities were not yours. Your secret knowledge of big impending change gave you time and space to dream, visualize, prepare.

You were by your *Self.* When was the last time you contemplated the state of your self—that which is essentially you or is particular to you, that which differentiates you from everyone else. Your self is made up of many elements that need to be cared for—your health, your spirit, your energy, your self-expression. These are the many parts that make you happy and whole. As mothers, we have finely tuned radar for noticing when a child doesn't quite seem herself or a husband is being selfish. Many of us fail to notice our own selves, unless it is to glorify our extremes of selflessness, as we achieve the daily rigors of tending to the souls in our charge. Even our most basic needs and wants are sometimes accommodated only with guilt.

A great Unpregnancy requires that you take time to be alone and to explore. Consider your body and soul brand new. What if? How will your goal—pursuing it and achieving it—change your life? What could you be like in nine months? Slimmer, stronger, healthier, sexier? Relaxed, happy, at one with your spirit, at peace. Expressive, funny, singing, laughing, creating.

Begin by keeping your Morning Journal and really listening to yourself. Let yourself have what you need. Let yourself be who you are. Not just who you've become or who others expect you to be. There's a little you who might be ignored in the face of the big you you've become—the grownup, the mom, the homeowner, the pillar of a community. Some roles fit better than others. Look carefully at your Self. (If you only keep a Morning Journal for a brief period, this is the time. Commit yourself to a trimester of sympathetic journal writing.)

You've just chosen your goals, so get started. If another important goal surfaces in the next several days, take time to explore both and decide which is important, what you need to do for yourself. In my own case, there were many ways I could have chosen to improve myself. My T1 Goals could have ranged from quitting watching *Law & Order* to giving up Solitaire on my computer, to getting myself to stick to a routine and write a novel. As I've said, what became important to me, what surfaced as vital, was losing weight in my first Unpregnancy and quitting drinking in my second Unpregnancy. You want your T1/Self goal to be something that is actually distracting you, bogging you down, stealing your oomph.

What you need to do most may be the one thing you're least willing to admit. It may seem like it is "under control" or not "as bad as," or "not my problem."

As I mentioned, I knew I needed to lose weight. My feminist self couldn't take that goal seriously (I'd read *Fat Is a Feminist Issue,* which argues that if you're busy changing your body, you won't have time to change the world.) At first, I considered it a shallow goal—because I was supposed to want to become a CEO or a senator or write the great American novel. I had to come to understand that weight loss *was* important to *me.*

Like many people, I was putting off other pursuits until I *lost weight*. I had to let myself admit what I wanted and accept it. Maybe it wouldn't be my most noble pursuit, but I had to start *where I was.* To quit stalling on the new me, weight loss was critical. I committed and I succeeded. I lost 50 pounds in nine months. As a stand-alone project, I didn't care enough about weight loss to stick with it. Understanding its necessity to my life's path helped me commit and succeed where I had failed in the past.

JOURNAL ENTRY

I want to take time now to find out what I want from this life. I guarantee you I cannot find that in the bottom of a Fritos bag. When I quickly eat the kids' macaroni and cheese so I won't notice or stop myself, I'm wasting my power and energy. Very soon after that buttery mouthful, I'm going to expend positivity to pull out of my regretful state.

Does Size Really Matter?

Like me, many mothers choose to diet as their first trimester goal. It's a knee-jerk reaction in America. According to the National Institutes of Health, more than a third of us are obese and 64 percent of us are overweight. This obesity factoid is widely reported by slim anchorwomen and other beautiful people on over 150 channels, with footage of lumbering fat people eating as they walk. (Being overweight means having a BMI above 25; to be considered obese, above 30.) Unpregnancy was the first approach to weight loss that I have ever used with long-term success. Unpregnancy is not an eating plan or a manifesto for weight loss. I simply noticed that everything that pregnancy gave me psychologically fostered a healthy and positive approach to my body and body size. And it helped me maintain a nine-month commitment to self-love.

Whatever your size, you need to find a way to love your body. If your days are caught up in despair about your body, you need to address the feeling, perhaps before finding a "fix" for the body fault. We are not Stepford wives. We have moods, bulges, attitudes, and occasional splurges. We have imperfect noses and unkempt hair. That makes us human, lovable, and attractive in the real sense of the word. We attract to ourselves real people who love us. Each flinch against our media programming makes us real. We don't need to be movie star gorgeous to be the star of our own lives. (Yes, in certain circles I am *the* Julia Roberts.)

I have been fat and I have been thin. (Thin is better.) My body has drawn scorn and ridicule and at other times actual applause (for weight loss). But inside there is always me. Who I am is not what I weigh.

Goal Wise

Make sure you're goal wise. You picked a goal, so stick with it if it is indeed something vital to you. You may need to look inside. What you believe is problematic behavior could actually be a coping mechanism. Some people clean when they don't want to confront issues or face discussions. Some sleep when they're depressed. Some people are addicted to exercise. Some people pick a fight or yell at their kids. Some people eat; some people starve. Some people drink, others smoke. Some use drugs to play. Some storm out and drive.

Then they feel guilty. Consider this cycle: Something scares you or makes you angry or anxious and you respond with behavior that shames you. You feel guilty. You feel so bad that you don't see (or have to see) the original scary thing. Now you're consumed with guilt, which seems to obliterate the original negative thought. Next time you find you're responding to stress with poor behavior followed by guilt, let it to be a clue to what you're trying not to see. Recurring guilt is a sign that you need to make a change in your life. You're covering up something that irks you. (You can read all about it in your Morning Journal.)

Is it OK in your life to use food as entertainment? Are you fighting compulsions and addictions on other fronts? Are you afraid to react with emotion, instead of food/cleaning/sleeping/drinking/smoking? It's hard to be yourself when you're no longer regulated by candy bars. What are you covering up, what do you consider unpresentable about yourself?

Compulsions are not all bad. They're a clue to repressed feelings. An undeniable driving force can be channeled into your mission, into your success. It can be a secret weapon. *Remember always to use your powers for good, Wonder Woman.*

GOAL CHECK:

* Whatever your undertaking, consider the problem at its base. How does it disturb you?
* How does it drive your life?
* How will fixing it help you?
* How important is it to you?

In this first trimester, you will look at yourself, love yourself and understand your new self in the context of your family and life dreams. Three lessons will help you launch your Unpregnancy in this trimester and help you revisit the earliest days of your first pregnancy. Remember how exciting, how purposeful, how inspiring it was? Your time is now.

LESSON #1

you'll never be alone again

She was not accustomed to the joy of solitude except in company.
—EDITH WHARTON

You'll never be alone again. EEK!! It's true. When you begin eating for two, you begin thinking for two, and living for two. And once you have a child, you realize that you have somehow allowed another person to walk the earth with *your* heart inside her. You feel so *vitally* connected to your child: The risks she takes—physical or emotional—engage your hope, sympathy, fear, and protection with more intensity than you'd feel about your own risks and endeavors. With motherhood, many of us have our first taste of mortality and fear of death or disaster—not for ourselves but because we wonder what would happen to our children without us.

Of course it is comforting to be needed and to know you'll never be alone again. Knowing the innocent and unconditional love of a child is one of life's greatest pleasures. Husbands and lovers may come and go, but kids are forever. Guaranteed togetherness can be very reassuring.

Once you have a kid or two around the house and you're trying to watch the news or talk on the phone, you might catch yourself uttering this sentence in despair: I will *never* be alone again. Mothers evolve from their first baby to the second and third. You can't bear to leave your first baby for a moment without heartache. With the second you're grateful for the occasional afternoon away. With the third, you spend some time each day *hiding from them.* Alone time grows in value; as your kids age, you get more time alone. And yet you know that as a mother you are not alone in the world. Your decisions are made within a nexus of possible outcomes, attitudes, and reactions for all the people you love and rely on and for those who rely on you.

This familial approach to decision making was first identified by psychologist Carol Gilligan, in her groundbreaking book *In a Different Voice: Psychological Theory and Women's Development.* Gilligan proposed and substantiated that women form their identities and values differently from men. Rather than showing a consistent application of abstract principles when solving moral issues, women tend to consider interpersonal relationships when resolving human problems and choose paths that "strengthen connections and minimize hurt." What essentially makes women *good*—i.e., moral—is that we worry for our loved ones and make choices that take them into account, sometimes basing decisions on possible emotional outcomes that men might find silly or irrelevant.

Gilligan explains that men and women have "two disparate modes of experience that affect their values and views of the world." She describes how women approach decisions, commitments, and their lives, all relative to their web of families, loved ones, and friends. It's not that they defer to others, but instead that they routinely take others' situations into account when managing their lives and decisions.

Gilligan contends that connectedness inflected with autonomy is the mature ideal, in psychological terms. It is therefore natural and valid for women to make decisions and life choices with their loved ones in mind. It is our instinct; we have been hard-wired for it since the beginning of time, quite possibly to ensure that we protect pregnancies, infants and families. This is one reason why so many of our personal goals are sidelined or neglected. It is why so many diets and self-improvement plans fail after a short while. We cannot do what we are often encouraged to do: *Put yourself first. Forget the crying baby. You can have it all.* All our striving, dedication, and success are enveloped by this invisible web. When we succeed, we want our web of friends and family to prosper as well. We do not want success at their expense; in fact, many of us won't even try to get what we want if it means putting the people in our web at risk.

Keep in mind how a pregnancy challenged and rewarded your family. Unpregnancy is informed by your pregnancy. In the same way that your pregnancy commitment thrived—because it was for someone else, someone you felt obligated to, someone you instinctively loved, *your newborn*—your Unpregnancy devotion will be just as strong as you coddle and nurture the small wonder in the womb: your new self.

Your adherence to pregnancy's restrictions and regimes came from a deep and true love for your baby and admiration for your new, amazing body and its abilities. You were driven by the new impressive role you were growing into: Motherhood. Now that your child is born, whether he is a toddler, in school, or in college, you still have a commitment to him. Nothing can change that. Unpregnancy shows you how to harness that powerful sense of commitment, support, and obligation. Allow yourself to enjoy having you as a mother. Nurture yourself. Encourage the you that is still unborn, still a twinkle in her mother's eye. You are not and never will be alone: your web of family and friends affects all your decisions. Like a fish being aware of water, you can barely glimmer your invisible web. You can't change your very nature. You can't divorce yourself from your identity and your values or from the loved ones who form the basis of those values. Your family can support your Unpregnancy, just as they have supported and sustained pregnancies in the past. And the new self that is emerging will astonish and enlighten the people who look to you for guidance and help.

Realize too that you are not alone, even within yourself. You are always every age you have ever been. You're the girl who played house and played ball, the college girl who wrote an impressive term paper, the 20-year-old who chose a career path, the mother who advocated for her children, managed a household, and planned a child's education. Every milestone you've ever achieved, every heartbreak you survived is clamoring for remembrance and honor. The person you fantasize about becoming—your ideas and dreams, wild, practical, or insane—is also within you. Those impish desires can be as childish and incessant as your toddler trying to get your attention and approval or as steady and responsible as your college graduate beginning an amazing career.

No matter how you feel about it, elated or exasperated, it is an immutable fact that you'll never be alone again. This makes setting goals and changing your life more complicated. It makes it easier to put your children's hopes first, your husband's needs first, or your parents' expectations first. This is why Unpregnancy is so important in your life. It is a way to get there. It takes each lesson of pregnancy—each pregnancy superpower—and gives it back to you and your entire web of supporters and detractors. All your many selves will be beginning an odyssey you've *all* experienced before, one you therefore know you can do again. Your commitment to your family is not going to change. Even as you work to keep your family happy and productive, you need to teach a true and sustainable love, not dependence. What you'll get is a chance to recommit to yourself. What your family will be offered is a chance to meet the many sides of you, from impish and demanding to sleek and powerful. They can accommodate your most inane ideas and profound fears to help you bring out your best, exciting self. Here is a life-change strategy they know how to support and indulge because they've done it before, too. You are not alone—you have your network, your invisible web. They're not there simply to demand of you—they're also your safety net. They are your midwives, your past, and your future. It is always easier to do difficult things with the support and company of people we love. Let them help you bridge from pregnancy and motherhood to Unpregnancy and Otherhood.

There's No Turning Back

As soon as you found out you were pregnant, you were committed to a family-in-the-making. You are obligated to your new zygote. There is no turning back. You can never see the world the same way again. You go back to your job the next day and every sentence uttered by a boss or coworker has a different implication to you. You talk to your mother and whether you tell her or not, you listen to everything differently. You're interested in very different parts of her life from before. Private or public, your pregnancy, like your Unpregnancy, changes everything. When Alice jumped down the rabbit hole to chase the intriguing white rabbit, she began falling and falling and she knew there was no turning back. The only way was forward . . . through Wonderland.

See for yourself what a wonderland your life can become by recognizing that there really is no way back—only forward.

LABOR #1: A LOOK AHEAD

Before I was Unpregnant, I was a: *(Describe **yourself** in your life now.)*

_____

_____

Now I'm a: *(Describe the most outrageous, wonderful life you can imagine for yourself.)*

_____

_____

_____

_____

_____

Imagine turning back. Every contract has a three-day cancel clause, right? So you're going to continue to live as you describe yourself above and give up on your Unpregnancy dream. You can't have that other life, right? It's too late; you're too old. Your children need you. Your husband won't let you. You're not good enough. Your friend is a better writer, speaker, dancer, painter, designer, (fill-in-the-blank)er. You don't have the time, energy, or drive. Your mother is always saying you're not ambitious. Why try? The truth is, you're already trying. You're already falling down the rabbit hole and Wonderland awaits.

LABOR #2: WRITE A LETTER TO YOUR OLD SELF

Write about why you failed, what excuses you will tell yourself, how you will rationalize your decision not to try, not to succeed, whose fault it really was. What excuses have you used in the past to rationalize not winning? What do you tell yourself each day when you disappoint yourself? Are you just keeping the peace, doing what others want from you? If you write this letter, you'll see some of the thoughts that help you fail. You'll see some traps that you fall into or shortcuts and outs you leave for yourself in case it gets hard. Then write a turnaround: Tell yourself how this will be different. This time you bring a different internal voice—kinder, more accepting, more expectant of yourself and others. You will feel the same devotion you felt in pregnancy, you will be your best self because this time you're Unpregnant. You will give yourself the gifts of pregnancy. Just as you devoted nine months to a healthy pregnancy and a wondrous child, now you will devote nine months to yourself, to your own health, and a trip of your own to Wonderland. You will use this Unpregnancy to become who you want to be.

(Begin your letter here and continue it in your Morning Journal if necessary,)

Commitment and Obligation

Nobody's a little pregnant. And when it comes to pregnancy, as with many other crucial moments in our lives, the difference between trying and succeeding is enormous. I remember trying. With my first pregnancy I had two years of "trying." Ask any dieter, smoker, athlete or entrepreneur: there is nothing more frustrating or exasperating than trying without succeeding. It is the ultimate stressor. It creates a sense of powerlessness and hopelessness that is hard to overcome. And yet we all face times in our lives when we come close—and miss it by an inch, by a few minutes, by 10 pounds, by failing to make a true commitment. The simple difference between trying and succeeding is commitment. If you're committed, you will see every opportunity, take advantage of each opening, look for every method to ensure success. You'll control what you can and compensate for what you can't.

A game lost in the last two seconds is devastating; the same game won as the buzzer sounds creates a frenzy among the fans. And once won is done, right? The winner moves forward, the loser doesn't. Winning is good. If you're in it, be in it to win it.

Even with the negatives of pregnancy, like weight gain and annoying, painful, even dangerous symptoms, you were obligated by your commitment to your child to fulfill your promises to yourself. Not everyone had the same promises or rules for a safe pregnancy, but most of us honored whatever ground rules we felt were important. If you felt you needed a nap, you took a nap. If you promised yourself no smoking or no drinking, you lived by that promise. You may have been tempted, but for the most part you didn't reconsider the rules. Imagine thinking, *I've been good for three months; I'll just take a month off and then get back to this healthy baby thing.* You were emphatic, even when it was unreasonable. And people you loved were responsive, even if you seemed capricious. Why? Why did you stick to a diet, give up things you liked to do? Why did you make sacrifices? Why did others around you make allowances? Why did you let some things slide that you normally consider important, like housework or weight gain? You committed to one important thing and you did it well. That commitment earned you respect from yourself and others. You deserved their consideration. With your Unpregnancy, you can have it again. It's not too much to ask: nine months for yourself, nine months to work toward something important for everyone whose lives you touch—a new vibrant self.

Successes create momentum and give you credibility and power over your own circumstances. The clock is ticking . . . there are 40 weeks to go. Make sure you're a winner when the buzzer sounds (and your fans will go wild).

Imagine your moment of success. Close your eyes and consider your moment in time. Visualize how it will be when you've achieved these goals. How will you feel when you get there? How will you react to the changes and accomplishments—with relief, pride, excitement?

Where will you be on your day of completion? At the Grammies? Hosting your own art exhibit? On a talk show promoting your new effort? In a classroom or graduating with a new degree? In a bikini in the Bahamas? In the corner office at a new job? Who you will be talking to in the course of the day? Oprah? Your estranged parent? The president? A talent agent? A class of new students? What will your successes bring you and your loved ones?

Focus

Like pregnancy, Unpregnancy gifts us with focus. One effort is more important than almost anything else. Most of us are juggling many calls on our time as we struggle to care for kids and parents, partners and ourselves. We keep houses and friendships, jobs and careers afloat in uncertain times. We fret about how to do this or whether to change that. We shop when we should write, eat when we should paint, volunteer when we should be building meaningful careers, work at jobs that pay the bills when we should be finding ways to fulfill our potential. We do something when we should do nothing. We act out of guilt, confusion, fear, and lack of focus.

LABOR #3: FLY'S EYE

In the hectic world we live in, our vision for ourselves is as splintered and disjointed as a fly's eye-view. Most of us have looked through a kaleidoscope to see many little hexagons, a fractured vision that multiplies everything and focuses on nothing.

Look at the 19 hexagons that make up a fly's eye in the diagram below. In each hexagon, write something that you do in a day. Start in the center with what you give the most time to. As you go to the next ring of hexagons, write in things you have to do on most days. And on the outer ring list what you do at least several times a week, anything that uses up your time.

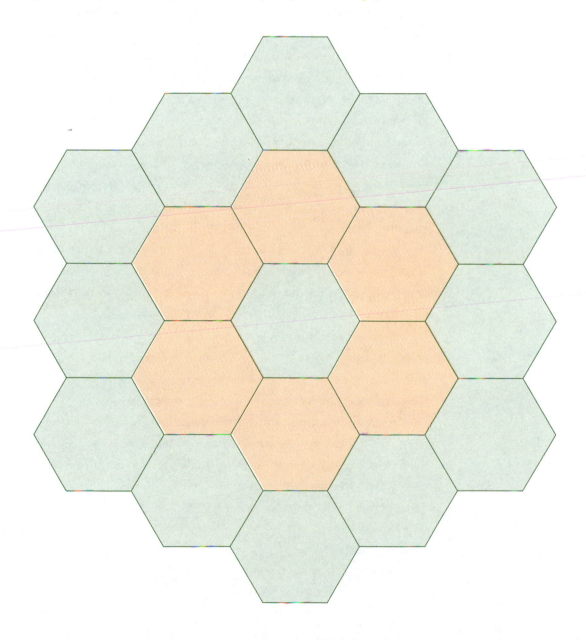

Look at each of the activities you're involved in.

❋ Count how many are things you want to be doing: _____ **out of/19**

- Beginning with your Unpregnancy, practice saying *No* more often. Cancel obligations. Say *No* unless it furthers or supports your Unpregnancy goals.
- *No* can be a very positive statement. *No*, I won't jeopardize my goals. *No*, I can't help both you and myself today.

❋ How many activities do you want to be doing more?_____**/19**

- Find two to three times a week that you could increase those activities. Consider this time equal to the time you spent in a Lamaze class. You found time for those classes, right?

❋ How many activities do you want to be doing less? _____ **/19**

- Find a way to do these less, simply put. Whether you find someone else to do them or they just get done less often, focus on minimizing their negative impact on your day. If someone objects, remind them you're Unpregnant and enlist their help.
- Once you whittle down the unnecessary unpleasant activities, you'll find you actually enjoy the ones you're obligated to continue doing.

❋ How many are activities that represent something for you? Something for your future? _____ **/19**

- Circle those activities. Are they within the scope of your Unpregnancy goals or simply something you wish for? If you're working toward too many changes at once, they might all be compromised. If you're passionate about these activities, consider fitting them into your Unpregnancy goals.
- One organized mom got out three highlighters. She used an orange highlighter for her self-oriented daily tasks. She continued to color code with yellow for things that were family-oriented, green for things that were work-oriented. What she saw illustrated was how little her life was about her!

  How many of your tasks are self-oriented? _____ **/19**

  __family/friend-oriented?_____ **/19**

  work/community-oriented? _____ **/19**

❋ How many support your Unpregnancy goals?_____ **/19**

❋ How many are distracting or harmful to those goals? _____ **/19**

I fill out a Fly's Eye chart every couple of weeks to ensure that my focus and time is invested toward what I really want. If I focus, I can create a living, breathing new life—my own—in nine months. If I can't, I'll have no one to blame but myself. I need to honor my vision and keep it focused.

Connectivity

We've established that women are social deciders by nature. We think and decide based on how our actions will affect a network of our loved ones (our safety nets). Our invisible web of obligation can make it seem impossible to change our lives monumentally. It's true that we're bound to *this* life, this group of people. But just as pregnancy and birth brought a new life to your family and was supported by your entire network of people, Unpregnancy can be a simple way for everyone to understand metaphorically what you're trying to gain, what gifts you and your family will receive, as well as what you might expect from them for a brief nine months.

Your network is as much a resource as it is a burden in this endeavor. As women, we know that connectivity affects our decision making and our willingness to make changes. On the opposite side of that coin, however, connectivity gives us relationships we can call on and rely on for help.

LABOR #4: WHO CAN YOU COUNT ON?

Women tend to underestimate the value of the relationships they build and nurture. As an exercise, let's count the number of people in your network.

HOW MANY PEOPLE ARE IN:	NUMBER OF PEOPLE:
Your immediate family?	
Your husband's family?	
Your family of origin?	
Your circle of friends that you talk to weekly?	
Your friends that you talk to annually?	
Other relatives?	
Work contacts that you talk to weekly?	
Work contacts that you talk to at least annually?	
People you know in the town where you live?	
People you know in your work neighborhood?	
People you've done a favor for?	
Volunteers you've worked with?	
People you've met at professional seminars?	
People who would know your name if you called?	
People on your email list	
Your Contacts/Total	

Each of the people in your network is likely to have a similar number of people in their own networks. Therefore, multiply your total by itself.

Enter the number here _____ X _____ = _____ !!!

That is how many people you can expect to help you! All you have to do is ask for help. Your relationships are a valuable and accessible asset. The number of people you can count for help is in the *thousands or tens of thousands!* You just need to let your own network of people know what you're working on, what you need, what you would find helpful. People want to help and if they're given a specific opportunity, they'll go out of their way to do so. Think of how often you helped a friend or a friend of a friend or donated time or money at someone else's request.

——————————

I love my daughter, love her so much I'm amazed I actually
have to hold her in my arms, that she doesn't just stick
to my side, my heart heavy as a black hole, dense with love,
trying to suck her into it.
—KAREN KARBO, *Motherhood Made a Man Out of Me*

Our invisible web can drag us down or hold us up. It is always there to support (or distract us). It is why we can commit or why we may fail. You need to decide. Can you ask for this support from your network? Do you believe you are deserving? Will the members of your network make—or have they made in the past—the concessions you need to make your Unpregnancy a reality? Can you see what your success will mean, not just to you but to the people who love and look up to you?

Helping a child grow and be happy helps us meet a fundamental need, gives us proof that we are competent and loving. To grow ourselves, we also need to help our children discover the difference between love and dependence. We can love truly only in proportion to our capacity for independence. Teaching independence as we yearn for our own is a gift we can give ourselves and our children (and in some cases, our partners).

We may never be alone again. We are sustained by, and committed to, a great web of friends, family, and supporters. Let that web be your cozy blanket, your safety net, *and* your trampoline. Put a bounce in your step as you move forward in your Unpregnancy.

only you can do this

Only you can be yourself. No one else is qualified for the job.
—ANONYMOUS

My best friend from high school, Susan, married her high school sweetheart. Susan and Sam were committed to each other and to having a family together long before I could even contemplate creating my family. Despite early love and maturity, Susan and Sam were 40 by the time they were able to conceive their love-bug, Henry. By then I had married, had three kids and was looking around for my next big thing, which became my Unpregnancy.

Susan and Sam's story is not unique. Prolonged infertility is a heartbreak many couples live through. And my heart goes out to them. Susan's experience, however, gives us all a unique point of view on finding and honoring our mission. Pregnancy for Susan was a true calling. She and Sam had tried every expensive, painful method available. Imagine their joy when after decades of disappointment, she got pregnant "by accident"! Susan wasn't just committed to her pregnancy—she was *über*-committed. After six months, she left the teaching job she loved, even though there weren't any specific complications forcing her to make that choice. Can you blame her? She wanted to be a parent with every fiber of her being and she had some 20 years invested in trying to achieve that goal. She felt *needed* as an inner-city high school English teacher—the students loved her and the other teachers were sorry to lose her—but she was *irreplaceable* in her role as a gestating mom for Henry. Susan knew this simple lesson: *only I can do this.* Her mission was clear: take perfect care of her growing baby and tolerate zero risk, even though it meant sacrificing other things she loved or disappointing people she cared about.

Pregnancy gave us all a mission to dedicate ourselves to. We got our own lives in order by making healthier lifestyle choices but we were also determined to make our outside lives better. Pregnancy acted as a divining rod in our lives and made many difficult decisions simple and clear. We left jobs or stayed in jobs. We bought houses or decided to stay put. We married, divorced, or reconnected with family. Big decisions were made easier by a defining mission. Big problems were easily solved because the permanent nature of pregnancy allowed for only one solution.

For example, I met a woman named Karen who had married into a family of perfectionists. Her mother and sister-in-law criticized her endlessly. Karen's style was hipper, allowed for more individual expression and was not as status oriented as those of her family members. For five years, Karen said she ate sh*t from these two, but she just kept her head low. Once she got pregnant, a new day dawned. Karen was having a typical family visit, enduring and ignoring constant critical commentary—when she began to tune out and think about her baby. She realized that she could not let her family treat her that way in front of her child and so she stood up for herself and announced her wonderful news in this way:

I'm pregnant and if you think you're going to be allowed to be this child's grandmother or this child's aunt, you need to start treating me better. Show me the respect I deserve. Don't keep trying to make me be like you. My child will love me and be like me. So you'd better start accepting me as I am if you want to be accepted as part of my child's life.

Her baby helped her define herself and fight for the family relationship she was entitled to (for her and her child).

⁂

This lesson is about finding and honoring your life's mission now, which are things only you can do. A mission identifies the strengths, passions, talents, and gifts that you have to give the world. A mission is what you need to pursue to be happy. *Always.* To duck your mission or to rein in or tone down your strength and passion is to feel resentful, disappointed in yourself, empty. The term "mission" might be a little misleading, since most of us associate that words with a strong, driving call, as in religious or artistic callings. Sometimes it's a word we use to explain inexplicable behavior, like why a painter would rather live in his car and eat Spam than give up on being an artist. We've all known one or two people whose callings were so forceful that they knew as children what they were going to do. As young adults they took risks and made it happen, while most of us took safer paths.

So maybe you've never jumped out of bed with a call too strong to ignore. And maybe you squelched a calling sometime in your twenties because you were afraid to try or because people said you had to start earning a living. Time to quit chasing rainbows, you told yourself. Maybe now it's harder to hear the call; it's more like a nagging feeling that you're not headed down the right road or a clear indication that the life you're already leading isn't exactly what you signed on for. Maybe you're missing something, a call that keeps coming back to you. Connect the dots: it's your mission. Often, once you recognize it you realize it's been there since your twenties and even earlier, waiting, hoping you'd heed its urgings.

There's a real correlation between having a well-defined mission and achieving success. Think about it. First, without a stated mission you won't consider it a success when you get there—and where's the joy in that? We take for granted what we do well and don't ultimately see it as a path to our own fulfillment. How often do we finish something and then undervalue it or belittle our accomplishments? You might apologize for what is characteristically you, when others see that characteristic as your special touch. What you despair of in yourself, others admire or even envy. Try viewing your quirks as your gift to the world, as part of an overarching mission. Then you can admire yourself and pursue achievements that you—and *only* you—can accomplish.

Imagine the 1939 movie *The Wizard of Oz* starring Shirley Temple, as it was originally cast, instead of Judy Garland. Both young actresses had enormous gifts to offer the world, but the world is collectively grateful that Judy—and only Judy—took us over the rainbow. Her gifts found a unique place in our hearts.

Second, without a mission, you will be distracted by goals or things to do that are not truly helping you to get where you want to be. And if you adopt goals that don't contribute to a mission—a mission you deeply and truly feel—you're bound to give up and fail. We try and fail so often because we get caught up in a cycle of trying and failing, of caring and not caring, all too easily. It's like running on a hamster wheel. Pointless, but we give it whirl, with the lame rationale, *Everyone's doing it. This diet seems to work.* Diets don't work, dieters work. If you choose to work at something, make sure it matters. Don't try what's not important. Get off the hamster wheel and make sure you're moving in a forward direction. All the work you do—at home, at your job, in your neighborhood—can and should reflect your calling. Otherwise, why try?

Sometimes trying makes us feel better about ourselves briefly. Like other forms of escapism—drinking, overeating, shopping—trying a new regimen can be a short-term salve for low self-esteem. Trying can also be a façade to hide behind. (*I tried. It's not my fault it didn't work.*) Why try without commitment? It's time-wasting and torturous. Repeated failures can leave us feeling just as sheepish and hungover as other escapist indulgences.

Any chance of success, which is what makes the effort worthwhile, comes from commitment. And deep down, commitment comes from a zeal borne of a personal mission. Ambition comes from inside, from having a mission that is uniquely yours. It is about finding what you truly love, what you're willing to fight for, and what will make you happy to get there.

You may feel you don't have an original calling, a singular vision, or a genius worthy of the word "mission." It can seem like a lofty goal. I counter your protests with a resounding, *Everybody does.* You have to find your mission and listen to it. Don't be afraid of it; instead, let it fill your life with purpose. Not everyone's mission is as public or as noble as Mother Theresa's. Successful people can usually point to a moment when they identified clearly what they wanted or had a vision that made the mission of getting there easier and the hardships along the way bearable.

So to begin with, your mission is to find your mission. Your mission is a defining purpose in your life. It's made up of what you want most, what is important to you, or what you do anyway, but maybe don't consider a true calling in your life. For example, my friend Mary was a matchmaker. She loved talking to people and telling them about other people she knew. Even though Mary's own career was stalled, she had helped most of her friends find jobs or meet important people in their industries. She couldn't help herself. She chatted with everyone she met and had an idea for everyone in need. Once, at a party, she got one friend an actual job offer from another friend on the spot. It then occurred to Mary that *people should be paying her for this service.* And of course, now they do. She's a successful and truly happy recruiter. Was becoming a recruiter her life's mission? Not necessarily, but it's true to her obvious mission—helping people connect. She now supports her family by doing something she has a gift and love for—matchmaking. Her office is a happy, productive place and she comes home enriched in more ways than one.

When you were pregnant, you felt you were fulfilling a mission. At least once, you thought with awe: *This is what it's all about*. Perhaps you were not as single-mindedly dedicated as my friend Susan, but certainly you were no less awed and sincere in your devotion. Being pregnant was part of a life mission. You wanted a family to be part of your life, in the big picture. Now, the question is what else can be in the picture—for you?

Who are you? What do you love? What do you secretly think you could do well if given half a chance? What are you righteous about? I mean, true zeal! Any good zealot is a friend of mine. If you're wearing your heart on your sleeve, you're in the right place. I love people who know their passions.

The only way to define yourself and see your mission is to see yourself as lovingly as a best friend would. Imagine looking directly into the light of what makes you great. We all need to feel great, but greatness is hard to see in ourselves. We need it like the sun, though we might eclipse our view of it purposely. We fearfully create a total eclipse of our greatness. How can you look safely into your bright, white greatness and see your mission? Make a pinprick in a piece of cardboard and let's get started. You need an eclipse viewer.

Find Your Mission

Let's view the eclipse. You will need to be honest and unabashed about who you secretly know yourself to be. For better or for worse, I know I am quick on my feet verbally. (Perhaps I don't self-edit well.) I know I'm funny (sometimes even when inappropriate). I know I'm casual and down-to-earth (even when conservative and reserved might serve me better). We are each unique. Our strengths are also our weaknesses. We just notice them more when they're working against us. And out of politeness, we might belittle our strengths even when they propel us to a great success. I know there have been times when my skills—humor, honesty, and a willingness to articulate an issue—are precisely what won the day and no one else could have pulled that off.

My calling—and, for that matter, yours—is to put yourself in places where your greatness is appreciated, called for, and *necessary* to get that job done. That is where your mission lies. Get involved in projects in which your passion makes the difference between success and failure or enthusiasm and boredom. You need to allow yourself to hear your calling, see your mission, and live the life you were meant to live.

For a moment, forget your loved ones. Forget your age, forget your job, forget your shortcomings. Put aside your many obligations. Try to open your mind and allow yourself to *see* what you are. Of course you deserve that. The exercises below will help you navigate toward your passions. Once you identify your central mission, it can be tailored to your life circumstances. But for once, see your mission in all its glory. Chase your greatness and do not allow your fear to eclipse it. To the best of your ability, look directly into the sun.

LABOR #5: WHAT GETS TO YOU?

List 3 hobbies that you enjoy, used to enjoy or have an interest in pursuing.

1. _____

2. _____

3. _____

If you don't have time for the news, cite three topics that still get your attention.

1. _____

2. _____

3. _____

Ask three friends to tell you three things that you get excited about.

1. _____	1. _____	1. _____
2. _____	2. _____	2. _____
3. _____	3. _____	3. _____

List three things that make you hopping mad.

1. _____

2. _____

3. _____

Write three accomplishments in your life that you celebrated, other than birthdays and anniversaries.

1. _____

2. _____

3. _____

Recall three recent activities that you got involved in that you just loved.

1. _____

2. _____

3. _____

What are your secret talents? Think of something you bring to every encounter that you know contributes significantly, even if the task could have been completed without that talent. Some examples might include kindness, consideration organization, humor, social skills, feminism, diligence, fashion expertise, a graphic eye, recruiting skills, a measured approach, or financial acuity.

1. _____

2. _____

3. _____

Look over all your responses to find unifying threads. Allow a friend to look over your responses and ask her opinion of what comes up repeatedly. Your mission is made up of those interests and facets of yourself that keep popping up.

LABOR #6: MISSION IMPOSSIBLE?

Finding and articulating your mission is not easy, but if you keep at it you'll succeed. You may need to write it down and say it out loud several times before it seems right to you. Eventually it will be a good fit for what you want; it will describe the life you really hope for.

List the five parts of yourself that are always there, always at work, your personal touch:

1.

2.

3.

4.

5.

Now, write your mission statement. A general mission statement might be something like the following: My mission is to pursue a life that applauds and strengthens these five personal attributes. My mission is to find situations where my passions make my work exceptional and make the process enjoyable and worthwhile for me.

Now rewrite the above mission statement, inserting your own specific strengths and ideals. My mission is to:

The example from my life would be the following: *The five attributes that are with me every day are 1) writing/speaking, 2) creativity, 3) empowerment, 4) flexibility, and 5) humor. My mission is to work in a flexible, casual atmosphere in which my writing and speaking helps women and girls. I hope to laugh a lot and enjoy the process. My family mission is to encourage and develop my husband's and children's creativity and personal power.*

For help assembling your five attributes into a sample mission statement, go to www.unpregnancy.com for templates that can get you started.

Authentic Self

Authenticity is a popular word in self-help books and talk shows. It is alluring because it appears to mean that we can do exactly what we feel like doing, when we want and how we want. Living authentically requires that you honor your core self and become the best possible you. What defines "best" is not all the rules we've become accustomed to: how you dress, how much money you make, what kind of car you drive or how perfectly you keep your house or even how nice you are or how many hours you volunteer at your children's school. Nobody's perfect, but who wants to be? What's better than perfect? Real.

To live authentically you have to toss out all the set rules and live in sync with your mission. Work each day to understand and honor the real you. Reconsider your values and the rules you currently live by.

For instance, how much of who you are is really *you*? How much is your basic temperament or personality? How much comes from what others expect of you? How much of the essential you is derived from where and when you happened to be born and into which family? Each family has its own standards and traditions, passed down from your parents and from their parents and from theirs. Like Jell-O in a mold, we are shaped by a long list of circumstances and conditions. Each generation accepts the mold, even as they dent it, cut it, and change it a little to make it fit a new family. You're in your mold and I'm in mine. Yet there is nothing keeping us there but choice. The mix of nurture vs. nature in the makeup of who you are is the stuff of self-exploration; it is what you learned to expect from your parents and what you know to be true, despite them.

If you know your mission, you've already heard a true calling that helped you crack the mold. If you have the courage to leave the mold and adhere to your mission, you may feel unprotected or scared. If you keep an open mind, you may find that a lot of things you have held to be true are not true for you. Little by little, you'll create enough new data to reshape your mold to fit a perfect, authentic self—you. Everybody's mold is different, diverse, beautiful, authentic and contributes in a unique way to the world. An authentic life is a work of art.

My mission is to empower women and girls to achieve their own best lives. My definition of feminism has to do with every woman knowing it is her right to pursue happiness and not have that fundamental right trampled, belittled or taken away by more powerful people in her life. I want to see that women have power in their lives to fantasize about, pursue, and expect happiness.

In hindsight it's easy to tell myself that in writing this book my mission was obvious. But I've known this to be my mission since I was stuck in a marketing job, paying the bills, coming up with ways to sell women more soap, dog food, cereal, or snack foods or to get their kids to beg for the products of my clients. It seemed like an authentic life to me. It came from my feminist desire to have a career and to be treated like and paid like a man. My career was enjoyable and I certainly met, influenced and mentored scores of interesting and empowered career women. But my thoughts continued to go astray when I should have been working. I wanted to write a book and live my mission more fully. I wanted my creativity to be mine again. I was ready. I heard the call and I took action.

When you are pregnant, you are pregnant every day for 280 days. No matter what pregnancy meant for you in everyday life, it was *every day*. Pregnancy was with you, protruding, intruding *everywhere* you went. Other people's ideas, suggestions, or treatment of you and your pregnancy were strictly subject to what you authentically knew to be true for you and your pregnancy. You even chose your doctor to support your authentic sense of what a pregnancy is and should be. Almost no one was allowed to veto your opinions, ideas, values, or mission.

Early on, you had time to develop this authentic sense of what your pregnancy was going to be like in privacy because no one else knew you were pregnant.

Your Unpregnancy can be protected from outside intrusion in its early phase. Now is your opportunity to listen to your world through the ears of your authentic self. Consider how your mission might change your responses and feelings. Take note of places where your current life doesn't conform to your authentic life. You know where your life is headed now, but you don't have to share that yet. You can collect data and see where changes might need to be imposed. Take 30 days to consider where your mission might intrude on your life and expectations and where your mission will simplify your decisions. What things do you currently spend time on that don't conform to your mission? Which decisions can you approach more easily and resolve more easily with the clarity of mind a stated mission provides? Who will you need to discuss your mission with to gain their support? Which relationships and exchanges are evidently out of sync with your mission now that you've identified it clearly?

Don't Do What You Don't Have to Do

Only you can do this. Let's look at that lesson in another way. How much of what you're doing could be done by someone else? Maybe not as well or maybe just as well? So much unhappiness comes from being too busy to see *why* we're doing the things we're doing. Get rid of some of your tasks. Do them less often or pay someone else to do them. Free up your time and energy to figure out what you must do for your happiness and success.

We all have tasks we don't want to do. Even if you weed out the awful jobs, any mother is going to have a healthy helping of unwanted work in her life. Try to minimize this workload so you can move past your resentment of it. Do the tasks you need to do and rest in between. At least you'll get back the time you used to spend stewing.

As I was morphing and hoping to evolve, I found Friedrich Nietzsche's parable *Metamorphosis* interesting and relevant to my undertaking. *Metamorphosis* is an allegory about how to evolve in your life. Since it makes a brilliant commentary on Unpregnancy, I'll retell it here.

METAMORPHOSIS
A Parable of the Camel, the Lion, and the Baby

There is a camel, a simple beast of burden. She kneels down and accepts her burdens and obligations without complaint. The work gives her humility and experience. She does what she is asked and in between she rests. It's a simple, honorable life. As she performs the thankless tasks, she builds character and gathers the strength to metamorphose.

She evolves.

Dramatically, she changes into a lioness, whose fierce strength is feared and revered. Very soon after her strength becomes known, her power is seduced into many tasks—much like the camel—but now she must learn to say "I will" and "I will not." Her strength gives her the unquestioned right to say no and the responsibility to choose wisely. If she allows her fierceness to put her in the position of tyrant, she will never be happy or safe. Others will plot to dethrone her. If she is responsible, her strength can guide her to happiness and a position of leadership in which she is honored, served and respected. She will be ready for her next metamorphosis.

She evolves.

She becomes the happiest, most powerful entity. A baby, happy, unconcerned and living in the moment. She is reborn. She fills everyone around her with joy and pride. She is beginning the dance of life anew. With the strength of character of the camel and the responsibility and wisdom of the lioness, her journey will be fulfilling, momentous.

The parable teaches us that each phase of our lives is important for building toward our own metamorphoses. We have all been camels, entirely absorbed by our burden when caring for a newborn. As mothers, we all have power in our lives. Like the lioness, are we seduced into tasks without choosing wisely? Do we learn to say "I will" or "I will not"? We all hope to create a new life in nine months—not a baby—but a brainchild, our own new life. The baby is an excellent metaphor in the parable of what we all hope for. The baby represents rebirth and joy, new opportunities and optimism.

LABOR #7: THE CAMEL, THE LION, AND THE BABY

THE CAMEL

Describe parts of your life that are like the camel's.

_____

_____

_____

_____

Do you feel that your obligations are building your strength of character and giving you experiences you will value in the next phase of your life's journey?

_____

_____

Do you rest comfortably without resentment between tasks?

_____

_____

_____

THE LION

Describe your lion-like strengths.

_____

_____

Have you perfected the ability to say _I will_ and _I will not?_

_____

THE BABY

How will you metamorphose into the baby, the most powerful entity, whose work is like child's play?

_____

_____

I will feel relaxed, happy, fulfilled and like I'm living in the moment when

_____

_____

_____

How do you feel about the following statement? "When I'm fulfilling my heart's desire, all around me will delight in my success and marvel at my rebirth."

_____

_____

_____

_____

Baby Steps

These are momentous times. Momentous has two distinct meanings, as it refers both to living in the moment and being made up of memorable moments. Momentousness is an important quality of pregnancy that we would be fools not to wish for again in our Unpregnancy. Living in the moment is a joyous, timeless experience. We don't worry about the future because it looks so bright and so promising and because we are so blown away by where we are today, what we've achieved up to that time. There is no greater elixir than amazing yourself day by day and your Unpregnancy achievements can give you that.

We also look at breakthroughs as momentous. You might think of some of your learning achievements as breakthroughs. You're struggling, you may or may not be seeing progress, and then all of a sudden . . . you're doing it. Something sinks in and you realize that you are *doing it*. Something becomes momentous for you: you have incorporated a business, reached your pre-baby weight, hit a milestone in abstinence from an old addiction, received a new response from an old friend or foe, or gotten a grant or award. We sense that what we are doing now will always be important to us when we reflect back on our lives. It is momentous.

LABOR # 8: BABY STEPS

Consider baby's first steps—they are each dramatic and each step adds to her capability. Consider your own baby steps. You toddle, possibly fall, but the exhilaration of each of these moments will lead to achievement of your goal. Break down your goal into baby steps, into attainable moments, momentous when achieved. Make sure you notice and celebrate baby steps.

Your Unpregnancy Goals

* T1/Goal _____

   * baby step (what you've achieved so far) _____

   * baby step (what's still to come) _____

   * baby step (how you will finish) _____

* T2/Goal _____

   * baby step (how you'll get started) _____

   * baby step (what's a good midpoint?) _____

   * baby step (how you will finish) _____

❋ **T3/Goal** _____

    • baby step (how you'll get started)_____

    • baby step (what's a good midpoint?)_____

    • baby step (how you will finish)_____

Give of Yourself

Your mission defines what is worth your time and what is not. It helps you determine when to say *I will* and when to say *I will not*. It gives you a path away from simply being a beast of burden. As mothers, we are called upon to give of ourselves by our families, our friends, our schools and communities. How can we decide whom to disappoint?

Corporations have giving policies. They give donations based on strict criteria that support their image, their industries, or their employees. Retailers often give locally to build goodwill in their communities, and get publicity to attract customers to their stores. They give with a goal in mind.

You may or may not have a lot of money to give, but you probably donate significant time and money in the course of a year. To protect yourself and your mission, you need to have a giving policy—not just for your money, but for your time, too. Your policy should be very specific about what you'll support and why that meets your criteria and satisfies your mission. It is not about what you *should* be doing. No one can do everything they think is good. Give only to what fits your mission and your authentic goals. If you give your money *and time* on the basis of a personal giving policy, not only will you feel better about saying no when you have to, but you'll also feel better about saying yes, too. That's because when you give to what you love, your contribution is priceless. There is no greater gift than that of your passion.

LABOR #9: GIVE OF YOURSELF

Rewrite your mission here

_____

_____

_____

_____

_____

_____

_____

_____

_____

Itemize donations of time or money that you are giving now.

_____

_____

_____

_____

_____

_____

Circle the gifts that support your mission.

Consider ways to pull back from the gifts and time obligations that have nothing to do with your mission. Who will you have to call? When is a natural end date?

Is there a direct correlation between the gifts that support your mission and those that you enjoy? If, for instance, you truly enjoy giving in a place that does not meet your giving criteria, consider giving it up to make time for your mission. Or is your resistance a clue that your mission statement missed its mark by a smidge? If you hate to give it up, it could be an unacknowledged passion and it may need a place in your mission statement.

Accountability

Only you. You are responsible for your own outcome during Unpregnancy. Just as in pregnancy, not everything is in your control. You cannot guarantee success, but you can do as much as you did during pregnancy to ensure a positive outcome. Your mission is something only you can do. Only you can live your life the way you dream it. You have a responsibility to yourself to give yourself the best chance at happiness and a rich full life. You have a further responsibility to your children to show 'em how it's done!

No one can meet your goals for you. As much support and attention as a pregnancy or an Unpregnancy might garner, ultimately it's up to you. You have to try, work, and succeed. Only you gave birth and only you can make your Unpregnancy a fruitful labor.

you are great, with child

A child's hand in yours! What tenderness and power it arouses.
You are instantly the very touchstone of wisdom and strength.

MARJORIE HOLMES

Great with child connotes enormity in pregnancy, but in Unpregnancy it promises glorious achievement. *Great, with child*, indicates that your child will always be a presence and priority, no matter how great you are. Jackie Kennedy Onassis is famous for saying, "If you bungle your children, nothing else you do matters much." As mothers, children are our gift and burden. They gift us with a childlike outlook, pleasure in small moments and perspective on what's important. They can also give us empathy and help. Do not underestimate the help your child (of any age) can give you to unlock your greatness, your joy, gratitude, awe, and wonder. Children typically have easy access to these happy feelings. These altered states are also gifts from pregnancy that we can recapture in Unpregnancy in order to feel "great."

Some Unpregnant women are born great and others have greatness thrust upon them. You are choosing Unpregnancy and seeking greatness in your life. Accept the greatest gifts of mood and outlook that pregnancy has to offer, the same joy, positivity, gratitude, awe, and wonder. Accept the easy knowledge that what you are doing is great.

We are *great*. I am, you are, we are *all* pretty great. If they heard a bald statement about their greatness, most women would say, "Oh, no, not me. I'm not great." First, there is no need to protest (I don't even know you). Allow yourself a moment to consider the possibility. Second, it is not *my* opinion about your greatness that makes it so (so why deny your own greatness?). Third, whether or not you believe it—secretly or openly—everyone reading this sentence *is* great. As women, as mothers, as role models, and as people who are striving to be better, we can have no greater human experience. This is as good as life gets. We are trying and succeeding, we are dreaming and hoping to find a path to that dream. We are pushing ourselves and we are delivering. We are regarding our own greatness with comfort and joy and knowing we can expect even greater things from ourselves next time. We are wowing ourselves with confidence and pleasure.

Most women would at least be willing to admit they are good. *I'm a good woman. A good mother.* If you find yourself agreeing to "good," but still feel uncomfortable with "great," then bear in mind how great goodness is. As Fred Rogers told us in *The World According to Mister Rogers,* "If you could only sense how important you are to the lives of those you meet. . . There is something of yourself that you leave at every meeting with another person." Good is more than good enough; good *is* great.

It is important to allow yourself to celebrate your greatness even as you also give nod to its context. You are great, with child. How did you feel when you first realized you were pregnant? *Great.* How about when you heard the heartbeat, saw the sonogram? *Greater* still. Then after hours of labor and pushing, understanding what your body could do, seeing the reverence in the faces around you and finally holding your tiny newborn, how do you remember feeling? You were great, with child. You had persevered, you had delivered, you had done something you never knew you were capable of. You had amazed everyone. You could see it in their faces. And when you looked in your baby's eyes, you saw hope, expectation, and a future filled with possibility and joy.

This remembrance of pregnancy and birth can teach us to honor what we've achieved. There is no need for modesty. It was a miracle (one of many in your life that you may or may not be willing to own as miracles). Within a few days of your baby's birth, you were ready to accept that women give birth every day, that what you did wasn't so very special. Even as you nursed, bonded with, and loved your new baby, you came to believe it was only special for the two of you. As you learned to trust yourself and knew you could see to her every need, you experienced joy, wonder, and awe. Nothing short of a miracle. It may happen in the U.S. almost eight times a minute, but the more you honor what you've experienced and achieved, the more gifts you can retain from this *unique* experience.

It is the same with our momentous achievements *outside* the labor room. We all have those moments, those times when we've worked long and hard for something and in a moment, life changes—we win, succeed, or triumph.

Even if a team of people stood behind you, supported you, partnered with you, you know *you* made it happen. You amazed yourself. Later, as you came down from the high, you undoubtedly heard about others who outflanked your accomplishment: for example, someone who opened her own business, helped an autistic child say his first words, ran a marathon, got a law changed, wrote a novel, or founded an organization. These are great achievements and some are perhaps greater than yours. The beauty of miracles however, is that like children, each is unique, life-altering, empowering and momentous.

Joy

Improving yourself is supposed to be painful, right? *No pain, no gain* is the motivational mantra. Changing your life is hard and taking risks is scary. Admitting your ambitions is . . . obligating. Don't tell anyone and you won't have to try. So how do you get to that place where in a moment you can bridge those troubled waters? How can you overcome fear and pain and see a clear path? I believe it comes from joy.

Why do we need joy? What role does it play in ambition and success? People achieve great things without joy, don't they? Joyless achievements are not what Unpregnancy is about. I'm assuming that if you're a mother, you're not inexperienced in life. I'm sure we all have earned many achievements—awards, plaques, and trophies—that are meaningless to us. Some of us built careers that were highly successful, yet brought us no joy. Some of us left careers before we could tell if they would have been joyful for us. Unpregnancy is intended to return to you the gifts of pregnancy—your uplifted outlook and sense of excitement. With these lessons learned and applied, your Unpregnancy and its life outcome will be a joyous ride.

While my own experience counts joy among the gifts and lessons of pregnancy, I realize that not every pregnancy in the collective experience of readers was pure bliss. We each had moments of fear, despair, anxiety, and maybe even dread. There might even have been times when we wished we weren't pregnant at all. Some pregnancies are harrowing experiences. What made all those tribulations worthwhile? Joy. Why suffer as we suffered? Because the heart wants what it wants. Our ambition to be a mother was fueled by the promise of joy. Unpregnancy is a choice, so make it a joyous choice. You are growing the life you always wanted! *What a rush!*

How do we increase our joy? How do we wake up each day enthusiastic and ambitious? What if we have all the comforts we could hope for, all the love we need, and yet not really enough joy? It may seem simple, but I say *seek and ye shall find*.

LABOR #10: FIND JOY

Find a way to ensure a belly laugh every day. The more you laugh and smile, the more buoyant you'll feel. There's hope in a smile and joy in a laugh.

* Find a book by a comedian, someone like Steve Martin, Ellen DeGeneres, even Erma Bombeck or *Calvin and Hobbes*—anything that you can dip into and laugh out loud.
* I recently finished Nora Ephron's *I Feel Bad About My Neck and Other Thoughts on Being a Woman.* I laughed out loud on so many occasions while reading that book that I went into mourning when I finished it. I missed my friend the book because it made me laugh. Consider it recommended reading.
* Visit a joke website. You can find a directory of joke sites at www.toplaughs.com. You can search by topic, such as parenting. Visit www.unpregnancy.com for a laugh with other moms or a link to jokes and quote sites.
* Tickle a child and let him tickle in return.
* Smile. It actually makes you feel better to laugh and smile.
* Permit yourself a daily sitcom, if that works for you.
* Crack a joke with a stranger.
* Steal someone's nose.
* Rent a funny movie once in a while.
* Get silly with a friend.
* Let your dogs crack you up.
* Play games with your cat.
* Dance.
* Write limericks.

LABOR #11: JOY DATE

Take yourself on a Joy Date. Go alone. This date is particularly important if you haven't yet finalized all your goals and need time to let yourself emerge so your creativity can bubble up. Go to a place you've always loved or somewhere you'd like to explore. It can be spontaneous or planned. Stop in a button shop you keep passing and permit yourself half an hour just to browse. Or sit by a babbling brook. Allow yourself to feel contented, happy, and alone but not lonely.

One mom, Diane, reported that she arrived at an appointment a half hour early so she took herself to a nearby coffee shop. She ended up just listening to the regulars talk at the counter. She loved the colorful expressions and accents.

Another mom, Carla, said, "It doesn't have to be a big deal as long as you're free to do as you please. For me, it was a matter of getting someone else to pick up the kids after school and having time and permission to follow my nose."

Just break your routine and do a little something to find joy on a regular basis. For at least half an hour, revel in your Joy Date without guilt or recrimination. Don't allow yourself to be interrupted. Allowing yourself joy will give you back hope and ambition. And ambition that comes from a deep sense of who you are will bring you joy. (Full circle.)

Positivity

"Whether you think you can or think you can't—you're right." Henry Ford's insight is reiterated soundly in *The Power of Positive Thinking* by the late Reverend Norman Vincent Peale. Indeed, thanks to Peale's bestseller, there is a well-established link between positive thinking and success, from locker rooms to boardrooms, to classrooms.

Pregnancy has a naturally positive voice. The sentences that play like a tape in your head are much more likely to be positive when you're talking to your unborn child and even to her mother. Instead of criticizing yourself or harping on your flaws and failures, you're much more likely to be loving and kind, forgiving and positive. Your internal voice takes on a caring tone, "Hey baby, how are you doing?" "We can make it up this hill. Come on, baby."

Similarly, once pregnant, it is easier to quit drinking or smoking and eat right, even though you may have failed in the past. Why? You framed your goal in a positive way. Instead of stating in your mind that you need to quit drinking, you're more likely to think of it as "no wine for this little one." Or "I'm not smoking up my baby's perfect, pretty lungs." If you were to approach weight-loss as an Unpregnancy goal, you would be reminded of how you approached eating when you were pregnant. You were feeding yourself and the baby the right foods. If you slipped and ate a pint of Haagen Dazs, at least it had calcium and you'd be sure to eat better the next day. You were *forgiving and positive*. The typical torture tactics women use on themselves—starving or punishing themselves, unhealthy fad diets, laxatives, compulsive exercise— are out of the question during a pregnancy. And pushing aside those negative options gives you back the only effective way to diet—positively. Feed yourself. Be deserving of your caring attention, cooking and serving foods that you enjoy and help you achieve your goal.

Let your children set a good example (you are great, *with child*). Think of how much more effective positive motivation is with kids. "Quit whining!" never has the desired effect. If the child does quit whining, he is likely to cry instead. I remember an effective tactic that I used with one of my whiny children. I asked, "Can you use your happy voice? I love your happy voice." When you hear yourself chastising or whining in your head, ask yourself to use your *happy voice*. Don't worry if this seems forced or awkward at first. (Think back to how a kid sounds when he first restates a whiny request in the best happy voice he can muster. It's not very convincing, but you give him credit for trying.)

When you first become a mother, you understand for the first time that you and only you are 100 percent responsible for a good outcome. Kids cry. They push your buttons and they can push you around the bend. But you're the adult, so the outcome is up to you. How do you prevent the push? How do you respond to it when it comes? How do you create the right atmosphere? How do you motivate your kids? How do you respond to get what you want from them? We can't all control every parenting moment and always obtain the perfect child or positive response. At 2:00 a.m. on Day Four of little or no sleep, as I was trying to calm my crying baby and get back to sleep,

I faced the same demon child everyone has held at some time, in some place. I felt anger well up. I felt desperation as I looked into a scrunched up crying baby face. *I felt a song coming on*. It was the single best positive response I can recall in my life. I relaxed and sang. The baby heard my song and relaxed. She wasn't sleepy, much to my chagrin, but quiet and alert. From that moment on, in the face of inexplicable crying, I sang. And it worked for both of us.

Here's a clue about your subconscious that was discovered by Dr. Maxwell Maltz, author of the bestselling *Psycho-Cybernetics*. When you provide your subconscious with ammunition—i.e. negativity—it will load its guns and fire. When you feel disappointed or angry at yourself for a small lapse in your goal achievement or someone else reprimands you for a perceived failure, it wakes your subconscious which then begins to assault your self-esteem and your sense of success so far. In its effort to reestablish the status quo, it torpedoes your momentum and builds a catastrophe out of a small setback. Negatively framed goals—quit smoking, quit drinking, quit yelling at the kids—don't provide your conscious mind easy access to the solution. Yet they provide your subconscious the very tool it needs to plague you with urges to quit *trying* and to maintain the status quo instead. Your subconscious leaps into action to tempt you back into what it considers the status quo: *Wouldn't you like a smoke/drink? Go ahead and yell; they deserve it*. Keep the negative language out of the framing of your goal and you will keep it out of your subconscious, as well.

You'll be thinking and feeling positive in no time—in 21 days, to be exact. Studies show that's how long it takes to get your subconscious on your side—to begin protecting the new state of being as if it's the status quo.

LABOR #12: BE POSITIVE, YOU CAN DO IT

Write a positive mantra related to your goal.

* **My weight-loss example: I will feed myself. Enjoying healthy foods will sustain my strong, lean body. I will look better and I will feel better.**

* **My quit-smoking example: I will be free. I will be steady. I will enjoy my life smoke-free.**

Each person's framing of her goal language is personal. It could take you a while to really connect to the right words. Keep writing and rewriting until the mantra speaks to what *you* want, how *you'll* manage, and what *you'll* gain. Even if what you gain seems selfish or a little embarrassing (like a nice rear end), if that's a meaningful payoff for you, don't fail to make it part of your personal goal-framing.

The mantra needs to have a true "mantra" component as well. That is an easy-to-remember short version that you can readily say to yourself. By saying your mantra, you can stop your subconscious cold and fight the urge to compromise your goal. In the kitchen, when I'm passively ignoring my weight-loss goal, what pops into my head? **I will feed myself.** I remember my promise not to eat unconsciously. I can get myself to stop and make a healthy and satisfying snack or meal when I'm hungry.

Once you've written a very positive affirmation of your goal, put it where you'll see it at least a couple of times a day. It doesn't have to be out where everyone can see it. When I was quitting smoking, I put an affirmation on a Post-it note in my desk drawer at work. It could be in your calendar or in a kitchen drawer. Mine is inside my closet door.

Say the mantra in your mind or out loud at least twice a day for 21 days. The affirmation gives your conscious mind the positive method and rationale for adhering to the goal. It does not fuel your tricky subconscious with the words it needs to subvert your efforts to maintain status quo. Remember it takes 21 days for a positive affirmation to take root in your subconscious and begin engaging in supportive imagery of your changes.

Frame your goal with positive language. Underline the mantra, a short, memorable statement.

_____

_____

_____

_____

_____

Post your mantra. Say your full mantra at least twice a day for 21 days. Repeat the shorter version whenever you need to derail yourself if you're tempted to go astray.

Gratitude

Gratitude comes so naturally to a pregnant woman. The modern guru of gratitude is Sarah Ban Breathnach. Her bestseller *Simple Abundance* introduced the world to gratitude journals. There is nothing more positive than gratitude. And when you are feeling grateful, it is hard to feel any negative emotion.

Oprah Winfrey swears by a daily gratitude journal to change your outlook. It is not so much the actual task of writing down the five reasons each day you are grateful, but what it does to your day. When you seek five reasons to be grateful, you're aware of and appreciate each blessing as it occurs. You feel more positive, more squarely in the moment. If bad things happen in your day and you're having a hard time commemorating five grateful feelings, you're much more likely to see the silver lining once you record your positive thoughts in the journal.

If you feel your morning journal entries are petty and negative, don't despair. They're intended to relieve some of your negativity and angst and to spare you the burden of carrying around the mundane laundry list of things that weigh on your mind throughout the day. However, adding a gratitude element at the end of each day will give you the gifts of positivity and gratitude in your daily outlook.

LABOR #13: CHRONIC GRATITUDE

Keep your gratitude list for at least a week. It's a minimal effort that can change the way your day unfolds. It will help you savor the good things in your life and set you up for more of them. Chronic stress and negativity could

be replaced in your life by chronic gratitude and pleasure.

Today I was grateful for:

1. _____

2. _____

3. _____

4. _____

5. _____

Wonder

You are great, with child. Some days when I felt trapped on the couch with a suckling child for much of the day, I felt it was a wonder any woman ever achieved anything, yet parenting filled me with wonder; I watched with eagerness and curiosity as my child developed and I returned to normal. A new normal, a state that also caused me to wonder, *Who is this new me?* I felt as if I'd been granted new abilities and I wanted to test their limits and know my strengths. (Granted, long after I'd satisfied my own curiosity, my kids found new ways to test my limits and to know my strengths—and weaknesses.)

A child's curiosity is something to be encouraged because children have a natural eagerness to learn about their worlds. Adult curiosity, however, is often associated with nosiness and gossip. But we can't allow the bright side of curiosity to be taken away from us; there is still so much in this world we want to know about and wonder about.

At the very core of a productive Unpregnancy is wonder. You need to take time to find the things that engage your curiosity and wonderment. You need to be sure that the goals you choose are wondrous to you.

We teach and yet we forget to learn. Learning for its own sake comes from inborn curiosity and wonder. Mothers sometimes forget that there is as much joy in learning as there is in teaching. So much of what we learn is on a need-to-know basis. You learn about something—quickly, frantically—when it happens to your child. Or you learn about a misfortune and hope it will never happen to your family. As we shoulder the responsibility of a family, so much of what we learn seems to come in the form of a warning. The evening news chases away wonder and leaves us fearful instead. But there is so much in this world to be curious about—nutrition, science, history, heritage, mechanics, dishwashers that don't work, stocks and bonds, pop psychology, watercolors, hand-made chocolates—and so many avenues for inspiration. It's a wondrous world.

LABOR #14: FEEL WONDERFUL

List 20 things you would like to learn to do that are creative or that satisfy a curiosity. It could be anything from calligraphy to making soup, from learning to knit to painting. Do at least one of these wonderful things in the next several days. Keep your list handy next time you want to make a Joy Date or just feel wonderful.

Awe

Awe comes to us infrequently but powerfully. It is a mixture of reverence, dread, and wonder inspired by genius, great beauty, or might. Carrying a child and giving birth are awesome achievements. When I nursed my baby and she made rapturous eye contact and twisted her hand around my index finger, I often felt awe. This little beauty (who would grow mighty in her lifetime) left me awestruck. As we nursed and nestled together, our bodies fit together naturally for this very purpose, and I was dazzled.

When I began to develop my first Unpregnancy, I wanted to ensure that I reached for goals at the very limits of my ability. I wanted awe and wonder. I wanted to amaze myself.

How do we find the courage to approach tasks that fill us with awe? How do we choose goals that mingle reverence and dread? How can we trust ourselves to fulfill our greatest expectations when we have only ourselves as taskmasters? How can we believe that Unpregnancy will give us an awesome reward? If you approach your goals with joy, positivity, gratitude, and wonder, you will summon awe.

LABOR #15: YOU'RE NOMINATED FOR THE I A.M. AWARD

I am willing to bet that you have been in awe of yourself on several occasions in your life. To honor your past moments and moments to come, create a space in your house where you will pay homage to those achievements. It doesn't have to be anything as ostentatious as a trophy room or as superficial as a wall of fame; we're not focusing here on awards given by groups, organizations, or trade associations. This homage isn't even about the tokens of love and esteem that you receive from your children or partner.

You are nominated for a prestigious I A.M. Award, from the I Amazed Myself Academy. You are both the nominating committee and the person you have to thank in your acceptance speech. (Remember to say, tearfully, *You like me, you really like me.*)

Think of five momentous occasions in your life in which you amazed yourself

and list them here:

1.

2.

3.

4.

5.

Now—*the envelope please*—give yourself an award for these achievements. The I A.M. Award is a totem, a small item that reminds you that *you did it.* I have several totems on my desk. If you were standing next to me, you wouldn't think them anything remarkable, just trinkets, even clutter. To me they each represent how great I am. These totems can inspire me at a low moment, give me a laugh at my own expense when I get full of myself, stand as testimony to how I got here, and remind me of the learning and gifts of that achievement.

I have a cactus that stands about two inches tall and a miniature RV nearby that remind me of a family cross-country trip, one we made without my husband. (It was a little scary but in the end I amazed myself.) I have a porcelain doll named Martha that represents my 53-pound weight loss, which brought me back to my pre-baby weight. (I'd like to thank the Academy.) My miniature cement trowel and rake remind me of a great accomplishment a few summers ago when I put in a brick patio because I couldn't afford to have it done by professionals. I'm sure when I'm finished writing this book I will nominate myself for another I A.M. Award. (I'll have to surprise myself with a really great totem, but what do you give an Unpregnant woman who has everything?)

I honor my achievements by not taking them for granted, not compromising the promises I've made to myself, and not pretending that it was easy. If you choose to honor a few great achievements in your life with a totem, you'll remember to stop and honor your future achievements as well. And you'll realize how many miracles you have already brought to fruition. (See, you are great. I *knew* it.)

t1/checkup

In the first trimester, place a checkmark by all the steps you have taken to ensure a positive outcome for your Unpregnancy. Did you:

- ○ Register your goals and print out and sign a contract from www. unpregnancy.com
- ○ Find a midwife or form an Unpregnancy group
- ○ Keep your Morning Journal four to seven days a week
- ○ Define a personal mission and adhere to it
- ○ Seek the help of friends and family
- ○ Feel joy and accomplishment as you work toward your goal every day
- ○ Research ways to achieve your goal (get started at www.unpregnancy.com)
- ○ Allow your goals and your dreams to be awesome
- ○ Feel and internalize your commitment to your vision of the new you
- ○ Frame your goal and mantra in strictly positive language and repeat it twice a day for 21 days
- ○ Try a gratitude journal

Now reread the letter to your old self; how does it make you feel? Are you still using the tired old excuses and slipping up? Or does that old self seem further away than you expected?

- ○ Fill out a new Fly's Eye. Compare it to your original Fly's Eye (Labor #3). Is your day catering to your needs rather than the other way around?
- ○ Do another wonderful thing on your list (Labor #14).
- ○ Keep a Journal of tasks you need to accomplish to reach your goal (e.g. a food diary).
- ○ Track the measurable changes on a daily or weekly basis (baby steps)

in a family way

second trimester—love

Relationships often matter more to women than making money, having fame or pursuing a career. The second trimester of your Unpregnancy will focus on your relationships with partners, children, siblings, parents, friends and family. Relationships are a central part of our well-being. It's natural that we make daily sacrifices to safeguard love and we do so willingly and without hesitation. Some risks we don't even contemplate because we don't want to upset the apple cart. Consider the place love holds in your life. For all the sacrifices and all the nurturing, are you getting back the kind of love you want in your life? For some of us, answering this question may require the help of a therapist, which can indeed become your second trimester goal. My husband and I attended a marriage-counseling weekend as part of my second trimester and built surprisingly strong bridges of empathy toward each other in those two days. It helped us and it helped me to be happy and free to refocus on other things.

Love, the subject of song and story, is not always romantic or urgent. We recognize and value love even when it's left to simmer on the back burner. We need it and we cultivate it, and yet we neglect it at times. Other times our need for love is so dire that we forget to love and protect the most important person in the loving equation—ourselves. Love is a deep and meaningful part of who we are. And we can all get the love we want and deserve.

Unpregnancy cannot take the place of therapy with a professional, but it can give you the insight that you need to seek professional help, if advisable. It can help you identify places where your relationships are not supporting who you are or who you want to be. It can help you tweak your network of relationships by filling in gaps, repairing some broken ties, and putting the bounce back in the trampoline.

Using your own pregnancies as a guide, Unpregnancy can give you a method and example from your own life as to how deserving you are of help and support and how to go about getting it if it's lacking in your relationships.

During the second trimester you will begin your family- or friend-oriented goal. You will continue working on your first goal, but its path should be fairly well-established by now and its gifts to you—confidence, happiness, energy—are things you'll be ready to share. You should be feeling pretty proud of yourself. If you're committed, you can achieve quite a lot in 12 weeks. (In that same time frame, a fetus has grown a thumb to suck. Now that's the kind of progress you can feel.)

Traditionally, mothers wait twelve weeks before they share their pregnancy news, so perhaps this is a good time to share your Unpregnancy news. Tell everyone about your achievements and bask in their excitement and well wishes for you (it's a great cheap high). Tell everyone about your Unpregnancy and what you've achieved so far! Breathe in their respect for you. Since they're impressed, allow yourself to be impressed too.

Goal Wise

In your first trimester, you began to work toward a vital goal, an effort that required focus and change. You may have demanded more; you may have given more. As you changed, so did the people around you. Just as pregnancy can challenge, stress, or strengthen a relationship, so can Unpregnancy. It's important and perhaps a little intimidating; it's exciting and maybe a little scary. As a result, some relationships may need tending. The goal you chose three months ago may still be the right goal for you and if so, take a moment to restate it in a positive way so you can be sure of success.

❋ **Frame your T2/Love goal in positive language and underline the mantra. Begin to say it at least twice a day for the next 21 days (Labor #12).**

Give yourself a moment to test or reconsider your goal, so your commitment is firm. Consider your unmet love needs. Who are the circle of friends and family that you rely on? How strong, nurturing, healthy, supportive and loving are those relationships? Do they rely too much on you? Or vice versa? *Can* you count on them? Not just in theory, but in practice. How can you reconnect with the people you love most? Are you committing yourself now to the right relationship makeover? Are you avoiding a relationship that needs attention?

❋ **Who is sticking in your craw? That person may not show support of your growth or may make belittling comments.**

❋ **Is there someone who may be due praise and attention for the help and support he or she gave you during the first trimester?**

* You may feel emboldened and ready to revisit a long-troubled relationship
* Your first trimester goals may have reconnected you with or put you in touch with a new group of friends with whom you'd like to get closer
* You may simply feel more joyful and want to share that with everyone you love
* Growing awareness of a longer-term life plan could cause you to realize the importance of your romantic relationship
* And as they say, "If it's not one thing, it's your mother."
  Does your relationship with your parents or your in-laws need emergency treatment?

Even as you include your loved ones in the circle of your Unpregnancy, your goals and achievements are still for *you*. You can only achieve something that is in your control. Although you can't make someone else's behavior your goal, changes in your outlook and behavior will probably result in different reactions from your family and friends, especially over time. You can give more or you can give less. You can change your attitude or you can ask for changes. You can seek help from a third party. You can invest in a relationship or divest. These are difficult choices sometimes, but they might be the changes you need to make in order to be true to yourself and be happy.

Did you know that divorce is four times more likely during pregnancy and the first year of a baby's life? Or that the most common cause of death during pregnancy is, believe it or not, murder? Pregnancy pushes a relationship toward its most extreme expression, whether that means loving or loathing. I remember being blown away by the love and support my husband and I shared at that time. His consideration of me was proactive and involved and I took empathy for granted.

Think back to the way your family acted during your pregnancy—weren't they more protective, solicitous, and helpful? Didn't you feel closer to your mother and father? Even your children managed to amuse themselves when you were exhausted. Your mother-in-law took no for an answer and you felt entitled to call in sick once in a while at work. People supported you and you accepted their help.

This Unpregnancy can elicit a similar level of help, love and involvement from your family and friends. You need to ask for the help because this time you don't have the big belly to do the asking for you. It's important that you accept the help that is offered. Explain to your family and friends why it's so important to you and how it fits in your new life plan. This is your mission. Your loved ones will share your zeal and they'll understand that you deserve this.

Share the Love

Let's share the love and spread the joy.

Take out a sheet of paper and number it from 1 to 10 three times. Label the first 10 "Family," the second 10 "Friends," and the third 10 "Extended Family." Now write 10 ideas for ways to spend more creative and joyful time with each group.

Look over these ideas to see what is possible, what would be enjoyable, and what might bring you closer together. Do you already do some of these things? When was the last time you made this kind of effort toward your friends and family? Look at your family list again. Did you think to address your romantic relationship with your partner? If not, give him a separate list of 10 ideas. That relationship needs nurturing, too. If you were to suggest these ideas, would your loved ones be enthusiastic or would it be like pulling teeth? If your ideas excite you but don't get support at home, try asking your family members to do this same task themselves. Then share your lists and agree to try one or two ideas from each other's lists.

In this second trimester you're on your way; you're feeling like a new woman and wanting to help your loved ones catch up and participate in this great Unpregnant feeling. Visualize the pleasure it gave your family and friends when you first shared the news of your pregnancy so many years ago. Share the wonderful news and gift of your Unpregnancy with the people who matter most to you.

you're gestating
(everything else can wait)

How are you doing? People ask that question of pregnant women constantly. What they actually mean is, *How are you* being? Being vs. Doing. When you're pregnant, you are content to just be. Your *body* is doing. It is a blissful state wherein anything else you do in the day is just icing on the cake because you're gestating. That's your good deed for the day, so you're off the hook for all other expectations.

Once you've met the "doing" obligation, the rest is optional. You do at your pleasure. While you were pregnant, you may have done a little or a lot. You may not have enjoyed everything you were doing, but as every pregnant woman knows, you can stop, let go of expectations, put your feet up, and let the dishes wait. You can take it easy because you're gestating.

When you're pregnant you take "being" seriously, too. You fantasized, visualized, and daydreamed. When people asked "How are you?" the answer was fascinating to you and to the people around you. It is a beautiful gift— to learn to be—and a lost lesson of pregnancy.

"Being" is underrated in our society. Every motivational book I've ever read emphasizes doing, achieving, and winning and most recommend defining achievable and measurable goals. Perhaps because of our pregnancy experiences and our relational approach to decision making, women do not tend to see their personal goals in absolutes. We can be happy and satisfy a goal even if the result does not measure up. Women want to *be* happy… content… proud… fulfilled… respected… secure…entitled. They don't always seek to achieve a certain number—dollars saved, pounds lost, items sold—irrespective of what it costs them emotionally. Like pregnancy, our goals are not concrete: a good baby is not greater than six and fewer than eight pounds, *without fail*. A good baby is *our* baby in our new family. We believe in happy endings.

Like everyone, we phrase our goals in ways sanctioned by the motivational gurus (that is, numerically) but our internal goals are really based on how we will feel as a result of achieving that goal and on how our families and loved ones will be affected. And although we know that the end goal—

the emotional aspect of being—is more important to us, we still focus on the "doing" aspect. When we ask, "What do I want to do?" there's an immediate choice involved and we agonize about making the right "doing" choices. We believe that if we choose the right thing to *do* we'll *be* happy. (*Do I want to try managing a restaurant and spa? Or do I want to continue with my physical therapy career?*) We can get paralyzed with fear about making the wrong choice or doing the wrong thing.

The Sixties emphasized being and de-emphasized achieving. Overachievers—the Establishment—were suspect; people who couldn't just *Let it Be,* as the Beatles anthem advised, were belittled. Of course, respect for just "being" raised consciousness and gave us women's liberation. In the Sixties-era movie *Coming Home*, Jane Fonda's character learned how to quit doing everything that was expected of her and just be comfortable, free of constrictive fashions, happy and loving, and in the process was able to flee her married life, which had become a prison. In today's society, we have made a giant pendulum swing back toward the Type A personality—its perfectionism and its neurotic levels of achievement and organization.

There's nothing wrong with doing, doing a lot, and doing it well! There's nothing wrong with concrete, measurable goals. However, every Unpregnant woman needs to acknowledge that behind the quantity of the goal is a quality of *being* that is far more important to her and must therefore be integral to the goal. What pregnancy teaches us about *being* must be remembered in Unpregnancy. What we choose to do must lead us down the path to being all that we hope to be.

Vacantly "doing" your goals without protecting your "being" won't help you achieve those goals. The most important thing you can do is to gestate! And what does that mean? It means to hatch or develop gradually.

LABOR #16: JUST BE

Set a timer for 15 minutes. Make sure you are comfortable and your physical needs are met, and then just sit. Relax. Loll a little. Close your eyes if you prefer or focus on a point at middle distance. Use an eye mask, if the cooling or heating sensation can help relax you. Now, do nothing. Allow your mind to wander and your thoughts to stray. Think of nothing and everything.

Imagine yourself at different times of your life or in more recent situations. Keep your focus on just being. Do not allow yourself to visit your To Do list or to think about how you should have done something or what you hope to do. Just let yourself feel and fantasize.

Ask yourself, *how are you being?* Track your goals emotionally. How is your Unpregnancy making you feel?

One woman, Patty, told the group she felt *like a teenager—nervous, but in a good way. Sort of jittery. My husband jokes that I must be having an affair. I guess I'm acting sort of elated and I'm making changes that he's beginning to notice.*

There's a reason everybody loves a roaring fire, Niagara Falls, the ocean, a baby. You can look at any one of these natural treasures endlessly and effortlessly. Such meditation can help you disengage from what you should be doing and just be. Doing nothing is not an indulgence, it is a need. You need to find times in your week to do nothing. They don't each have to be 15 minutes long—that is simply a starting point. But if you arrive at your destination early or are waiting for a bus, if you can turn off the TV and stay put for a quarter of an hour—do it. You will find in these brief interludes that you can see how you are being, adjust what you are doing and make sure you are headed where you truly want to be.

False Labor

We are indeed human beings and not human "doers." Once you turn yourself into a human doer, you are merely a beast of burden. Remember the parable *Metamorphosis* about the Camel, the Lion and the Baby (Lesson #2, page 83). Like the camel, you are exploited, directed by others and unconsciously turning over your *being* to whoever directs your deeds. The camel is a noble being, primarily because she accepts her burden without complaint, performs her tasks and in between she rests. In the process, she builds character. Her nobility is in her lack of ambition, hope, or despair. There is no cause to foist a goal onto this contented animal. The camel is a doer, without choice or will—or hope.

There is certainly a time in a mother's life when doing is all she can manage. A newborn knocks her flat and her being is completely subverted by constant doing for this new little being. Only by doing the new baby things—

diapering, nursing, cradling—can we even come to understand our new state of being, as a mother. It is the needy newborn who directs our tasks. And like the Camel in *Metamorphosis*, most mothers of newborns perform without complaint; indeed, they feel contented and happy even if they can't manage to eat enough, sleep enough or take a shower every day.

As mothering continues, we continue to give and do unquestioningly. This is a busy time of life. We do so much for our children, our houses, and our communities. We may feel overwhelmed, but we feel that doing—being busy—is part of who we are, part of our value in the world.

You keep laboring and that is perfectly normal, but is it true labor or false labor? Even false labor pain can cause breathlessness, force a woman to sit down and elicit an utterly panicky response. In short, false labor is very easily mistaken for true labor. It feels like true labor and it wears you out in the same way. True labor is hard work, and yet satisfying because it's productive, but false labor is busywork.

The Busy Badge

If pregnancy brings the easy state of being, birth brings an unconscious frenzy of doing. It is a seismic shift from being to doing. By necessity, you give over to doing, lovingly, willingly, and without regret, and it feeds your being wholly.

You've earned your Busy Badge. You can hold your head high in the endless To Do list showdown that we all engage in. Who's busiest? Whose life is the most impossible? It's not enough that we are busy, but we have to prove it to other women. Why? To impress and intimidate each other? Does a complaint about being busy mitigate our arrogance about how needed or important we are? Do we use the Busy Badge to brag about our achievements? *I have to get my daughter a new dress because she's winning an award.* Is it martyrdom? Is it a defense? *I'm just too busy to help you with another bake sale.* Is it validation? After all, we *want* the Busy Badge. We never brag about going home to sit around, even if it's true, *especially* if it's true. Imagine saying to a friend, *I can't help you because I have scheduled some do-nothing time.*

And yet "busy" is sort of a derogatory word. It doesn't connote the same power as words like engaged, leading, active, building, productive, or effective. If I ask my husband how his day was, he never says "busy"; he says he had a very hard day. He can't believe how much he got done, how he moved forward, what he managed.

Being "busy" implies busywork, which is unproductive and insignificant in the scheme of things. A "busybody" is someone who fills her days with meddlesome nothingness. Being "busy" also implies that you're not in control of the busyness. Things keep you busy. Or you keep yourself busy to kill time, because of depression or grief or to stave off urges to overeat or watch too much TV. When you're forced to wait, like when you're pregnant and you need to keep your mind occupied so you don't think about the other, harder, real engagement, you keep busy

People strive to be busy, thinking it will bring them success. When you're busy, it means you're sought after, important, and needed. Every *successful* woman is Type A, right? Have you ever read a profile of a professional, successful woman in a magazine who is *not* a perfectionist, ultra-busy, powerful and in charge down to the last detail? No one who is anyone is ever identified as a Type B personality. (What does that "B" stand for? Busy helping Type A's?) The Type B personality actually exists, but it just doesn't get very good press. For the record, someone who is Type B is the opposite of Type A; i.e., she is relaxed, uncompetitive and inclined to self-analysis. Her sense of pride and self-esteem come from being creative, flexible, and social (in the Sixties, those types were the hippies). Type Bs have their own alternate version of success—it's called "being." If Type A wins in the **A**chievement contest, Type B wins in the **B**eing contest. As we've discovered, "doing" becomes mere busywork if "being" isn't attended to.

Type C personalities are the people pleasers, helpers, and self-sacrificers of the world. Many Type Cs are attracted to careers in the service professions, such as nurses, teachers, assistants and volunteers; they build their self-esteem through helping other people. Type Cs need to be especially vigilant that they take time to simply be. If her sense of fulfillment comes from helping, she needs to judge when to help as the lion in the parable did: *I will and I will not*, said the lion. Her power and gratification come from doing good in ways that fulfill her.

If you are a Type C personality, take extra care to give your gift of time and support in a way that builds toward a goal you desire and feeds your personal satisfaction. If you're helping others just to do with no regard for your own being, you may end up resenting others instead of gaining the self-fulfillment you deserve.

LABOR #17: FALSE LABOR

The difference between true and false labor is its product. Your labor, as difficult and all-consuming as it is, needs to be fruitful and to give you new life. Look at your To Do list. If you do not have a current list, create one now. Write everything down. Don't reserve the smaller everyday items in your head. Make sure that everything you think you need to do is on one list. Now look at your full list and circle the tasks that you will be glad you did one year from now, either, because they will make a difference in your life or the lives of people you love, or because they will build towards something that will matter to you.

> This is true labor.
>
> The remainder of the tasks—the false labor—may be tasks you can choose not to do. Write down the words "I will not" next to each task you would like to get rid of and then consider ways to skip or discard those jobs.

Anything Can Wait

Remember when you had a newborn with a nap regimen and then later a pre-K schedule with drop-off and pickup two and a half hours apart (plus a 15-minute drive each way and by then a new infant with a new nap regimen)? Ever since your first child was born you've lived your life on a timer. Ding! Time's up. Time to go. No time. Whether you clocked in at work or not, your life began to be meted out in increments. Ding. Get the kids off to school. Ding. Doctors' appointments, lunches, dinners, haircuts, school plays. Ding. Consult your Filofax. Set a goal for every 15 minutes. Ding. Set your alarm early to get some time alone. Ding. Catch a train. Ding. Chauffeur teenagers to the mall. Ding. Pick them up. Ding. Work out 35 minutes a day. Ding. Pay bills, manage investments. Ding. Ding. Ding. *If no one is present, ring bell for assistance* (nice notion).

You thought you were busy before you had children and then you learned what busy really is—demanding, challenging, flat-out busy. If you had a second child, you looked back fondly on your first pregnancy when you *could* nap or take a day off. Despite your pregnancy, you had your first child to care for (and it goes without saying, the rest of your life). But even with the level of demand in your second pregnancy, didn't you find that *anything* could wait? Even your toddler had to accept the facts: maybe you couldn't pick him up every minute or she would have to walk more; maybe she got kicked out of your bed at night to prepare for the incoming newborn; maybe he let you nap and napped with you; maybe roughhousing waited for Daddy.

If a toddler can wait . . . anything can wait.

You've certainly waited a long time to put yourself first. Ding . . . you are Unpregnant. Whose life is it, anyway? Anything can wait! Dinner, deadlines, details, demanding bosses. You have waited long enough.

Looking at your life now, with whatever level of doing it contains— toddlers, teenagers, aging parents, needy husband, adult children in crisis—be honest, do you rest between tasks? From having newborns until now, did you manage a time to be? Have you been at peace, have you tended to your happiness? Are you overdoing to avoid facing your inner being? Is your "being" seething under the busy surface, waiting for your attention, deserving your gaze, craving your support?

Ding. Gotta run. Ding. Can you find happiness in small increments of time? Ding. If anyone can, a mother can.

What are you busy with? Consider your Unpregnancy a hiatus. Many of our daily tasks can't wait 40 weeks, but many of them can be put on the back burner for a period of time. Maybe a friend or sister can take over or share some of your obligations for 40 weeks. Maybe you can consider this your sabbatical and pay a replacement during your "leave of absence." Hire your replacement—a housecleaner, a babysitter, a gardener, a handyman, a financial advisor—or farm out some of your professional work so you can have a little more time. Decide to have dinner delivered twice a week or put off a big project to free up your time.

Maybe you can weed out many of your time-consuming tasks—for at least 40 weeks—to give you time to focus on your needs. Some women, when they first become pregnant, quit their jobs, leave volunteer positions, and decide against an ambitious career move or a new house (regardless of who ends up disappointed). And then some pregnant women take on highly ambitious roles such as running for office, moving to a new house, starting a new company or deciding to compete for professional acclaim (regardless of who might be dis-comfited or shocked).

LABOR #18: BE BACK SOON

Pregnancy has a tendency to compress time and to clarify your desires; it makes it easier to walk away from dreaded obligations and embrace and achieve your heart's calling. We've all walked up to a shop in the middle of the day and found the door locked unexpectedly. Can't you close up shop once in a while and hang out a "Be Back Soon" sign?

What can you put on hiatus? What are you doing that can wait 40 weeks? (Examples: closet reorganizing, garden refurbishing, volunteering, social obligations)

How can you enlist support by telling people about your Unpregnancy goals?

How will 40 weeks of Unpregnancy affect your life long-term?

How will postponing these entanglements positively affect your life?

Will there be any negative effect on your life?

How will it feel to reclaim your time?

The Time of Your Life

Time, money, and closet space are three things we can never have enough of, or so goes the common wisdom. How do we manage to make, justify and *take the time* for an Unpregnancy?

The precise length of pregnancy is 40 weeks, the time you dedicated to someone else and the amount of time you've now earned for yourself. Because pregnancy is just 40 weeks, so is Unpregnancy. Forty weeks, 280 days—it's an important gift of time to yourself and sufficient time to make a dramatic life change, but not too long to conceive of sticking with a life-altering program or asking a family, friend, or coworker to indulge your need for time and support.

In smaller increments, it's 6,720 hours or 403,200 minutes. What life clock ticks off these minutes? How will you enter the Unpregnancy time zone?

What brings you to this Unpregnant time in your life? Was it a milestone birthday? Was there a big life event that reminded you of time slipping through your fingers? Was it simply your biological clock (perhaps it was your kids getting closer to adulthood?) that showed you how important it is to take time for yourself, time to build the life you desire? Or perhaps it was a growing sense of your own mortality, a sense that time isn't limitless and cannot be frittered away? This is the Unpregnancy time zone.

I used to work around the clock and handle responsibilities way beyond my experience. I was keeping all the spinning plates in the air and, in retrospect, I believe I acquitted myself admirably, but at the time I was literally working myself to death. I raced from conference call to meeting to press proofs to client lunches. I worked till 2 a.m. many nights drafting comments and client input for the next morning.

In those days, everything was urgent. I never walked; I always ran. I often fantasized about falling and breaking my leg just so I could escape the pressure. I was dying to know what would happen if I couldn't continue to run down the halls, speed-dial, gulp down three meals at my desk and think straight through the adrenaline rush. On top of all that misplaced dedication I was fired—five times. It was the only way my crazy boss knew how to say he was angry, nervous, concerned or unhappy. Obviously, I was also rehired on a regular basis, until the last time, when I accepted his escape hatch, and negotiated a generous severance package.

There were real-life object lessons in this experience, the first of which is the crucial realization that no matter how busy you are, if and when you quit doing what you're doing, someone else will step up (even if it takes two or three people). Secondly, even though I felt I never had enough time it turns out that I had all day and all night. I was just using it wrong. I had stepped through a time portal: time is better when it's yours. I also rethought the value of money in my life. I was well compensated, on the one hand, and robbed of my life on the other. It's like a cosmic stickup: Your money or your life. Enough money is better than more money, particularly when earning it is disproportionately destructive of what you want it for—quality of life. And I've since learned something else, too: like me, a lot of women who are under dire pressure—professional or emotional—fantasize about dying or getting hurt in order to escape the pressure. It is nature's way of reminding you of your mortality and telling you that you must take back your life.

All of us have time, money, (and closet space) issues. You're busy with tasks that matter to you and to people who rely on you, those you love. And that makes it hard to step through the portal into the Unpregnancy time zone. We hope to find the will and the way to make our 40 weeks, 280 days, 6,720 hours and 403,200 minutes *the time of our lives!*

Reality check: Look back at your To Do list and try assigning time allotments to the tasks you are committed to doing. Be realistic! I always think I can do way more than I actually can. I once told a friend that I could run up to the craft store and get the materials we needed for a Girl Scout meeting and probably still be back in time to meet the girls and start the meeting in 45 minutes. I calculated aloud: 15 minutes up there, 10 minutes in the store and 15 minutes back. She replied, *In what?!! Dog minutes? Get real. We'll do without those supplies. It doesn't have to be perfect.* Reality check! Check your time estimates and eliminate unnecessary tasks. Consider ways to make necessary tasks easier, even if that means they won't meet your "perfect" standards. If I were 15 minutes late to meet a group of fourth graders for a Scout meeting, they would remember that for a year (and their mothers would remember it to this day). That I didn't have the right color felt or enough glitter to go around passed unnoticed. That I didn't rush around like a maniac to make the project perfect was a true accomplishment.

Good Things Come to Those Who Wait

Everyone who's ever been pregnant knows that there's a time for pushing and a time for waiting. Neither will work when the other is so obviously the only possible effective solution. Depending on your personality type, you may be gifted in one but not the other. I typically have no problem pushing but absolutely cannot stand having to wait. I remember a high-strung bookkeeper named Ida at my first job. She could be very dear and I enjoyed her point of view when she was relaxed, but she took her work *very seriously*. When she waited for an elevator, she pressed the down button continuously until it came. She pushed and pushed when it was absolutely futile because she wanted people to notice her harried dedication.

Waiting can make you feel powerless and Ida's elevator button-pushing illustrates why: you are powerless. Your only powerful choice is to see and accept the wait. Once you've identified an unalterable wait, practice relaxing. There is power in letting go. During the holidays once I had the pleasure of visiting a Baptist church in Washington, D.C. presided over by a charismatic reverend and his lovely, devoted family. Neither my children nor I had ever been to an AME Baptist service before and it was a moving experience in every sense of the word. The music moved us to our feet as the celebrants clapped and the youth choir swayed and sang the gospel hymns. The world and its woes melted away briefly and we were united in optimistic energy even as we gave our tithes to help shut-ins and impoverished people in far-away places. We were empowered as a group.

The sermon focused on delayed gratification and resistance to temptation. You've got to wait for peace, to heal wounds, to reach heaven, to find love, to ask for wisdom.

At one point a beautiful gospel soloist, the reverend's daughter, left her fussy godchild in the arms of her companion and approached the altar. She took the microphone, looked out at the congregation, and allowed the music to begin. Then she sang slowly, soulfully, and beautifully. As we listened to the song's tale of need, pain, prayer, hope and despair, she captured us heart and soul. Her song touched me in particular because it drove home a weakness in me—the necessity of learning to wait in faith:

> *What can you do when you've done all you can?*
> *When you've cried and you've tried and you've hoped and you've prayed?*
> *What can you do when you've done all you can?*
> *You've got to stand.*

Her hymn was delivered with talent and passion. Her message resonated with me for weeks afterward and taught me a lesson I don't accept easily. You've got to stand.

LABOR #19: GOOD THINGS COME TO THOSE WHO WAIT

Open your mind to the wait. It will happen in your goal pursuits: a plateau in a diet; a delay in the response from a publisher; the wait for an appointment with a professional coach. Identify things that are not in your control and cannot happen when you command.

1. _____

2. _____

3. _____

Consider powerful ways to use the wait time. Rest. Work on a different project. Bond with people around you. Take a Joy Date or write in your Morning Journal. List some ways you can endure the wait time:

1. _____

2. _____

3. _____

List some things you can get done on your own during a delay:

1. _____

2. _____

3. _____

Women's right to vote was first called for in Seneca Falls in 1848. The noted organizers of that first Women's Rights Convention—Elizabeth Cady Stanton, Lucretia Mott and later Susan B. Anthony—sought to change laws for women about property ownership and wages earned in marriage. They began the work that led to a national movement to demand women's right to vote. Their goal took 72 years to accomplish and on that day in 1920 when women voted for the first time in a national election only a *single* attendee of that 1848 convention had lived long enough to cast her vote.

Our right to vote and thereby function as equals in American society is thanks to the iron-jawed angels (as they were called) at the turn of the last century who faced ridicule, imprisonment, violent attacks, and harassment everywhere they went—the suffragists. Beginning in January 1917, Alice Paul and Lucy Burns organized a daily silent protest on the steps of the White House. For months, Woodrow Wilson's "silent sentinels" stood on the White House steps daily, waiting for him to bow to pressure and ratify the Nineteenth Amendment for women's suffrage.

Good things come to those who wait. This saying is typically invoked to ask children to wait quietly. Sometimes you've done all that you can and pushed as hard as will be effective and you just have to wait. In pregnancy, you had to wait out those interminable last weeks. Patience can provide peace of mind for those times when you just have to wait. And when you learn to do that well, good things will come.

you don't know what to expect

When a woman is pregnant, we say she is *expecting* and all around her expectations change. The expectations of bosses, parents, husbands, children and friends shift. And the dramatic shift in the intricate network of mutual expectations happens so quickly that you can suddenly see it. An expecting woman has something akin to a sixth sense: she has a temporary awareness of the many expectations—her own and others'—that make up her life.

Under normal circumstances we make expectations "pacts" with people all the time without being aware that we have done so. We choose friends who are tidy like us or who will support our sloppiness. We turn to the *right* friend to complain when someone fails to meet an expectation because we know she will share our indignation and validate the expectation. We leave our children with another mother and trust that our unspoken expectations will be honored. We all expect things from our husbands, partners, friends and children many, many times a day—and vice versa.

During pregnancy, not only did your attitudes shift, but all around you people seemed to be making new assumptions. And you were much more aware of those assumptions and expectations because they were *new*. Strangers touched your belly, asked about your health, gave you unsolicited advice, and told you to take it easy. Your friends and family had ideas and expectations that they presumed you would share. We make spoken and unspoken assumptions about pregnant women and birth all the time. *She'll have to quit her job. She'll be moody. She'll be beautiful. She'll be weak. She'll be strong.*

Some of these new expectations we agreed with (we'd nod, smile and say *I know*) and some we did not. If not, we resisted, redirected, or insisted on a different line of questioning or an attitude adjustment, sometimes tactfully and sometimes forcefully. Our new group of expectations had to be iterated and we felt passionately about getting it right and telling people what was right for us. Rachel is a lovely, soft-spoken, and diligent woman. As an architect, she dealt with high-strung, pampered clients whom she prided herself on being able to handle. She herself was low maintenance. During her first pregnancy, instead of putting up her feet or demanding attention and service, as people around her expected, she put on a hard hat, went to the work site and told every contractor or foreman who tried to give her special attention, "Ignore the belly." Pregnancy was an occasion for her to firmly establish her identity as a capable, reliable, and dedicated architect. Though her family and coworkers considered coddling in her condition to be warranted, she wanted to establish her own expectations of the pregnancy—business as usual.

Expectations about pregnancy are shaped by our families, but also by books, doctors, TV, and magazines. We talk to everyone we know who's ever been pregnant and pore over countless books and articles. We witness anchorwomen, celebrities, and runway models going through the comical, unexpected body convolutions of pregnancy. We consult our moms and aunts who can vaguely remember being told not to drink water or to go ahead and smoke. Given what we hear from each of these sources, we temper our own expectations and we keep an open mind. We research, we ponder, and we weigh the sources. We come away with our new set of expectations:

I will be tired. I will feel strong and purposeful. I will be delicate; I will have morning sickness. My emotions and hormones will be out of whack. I should exercise and quit horseback riding. My husband will be so caring of me; I won't be interested in work anymore. I will have cravings. I will take good care of myself, get my rest. I can do it all. My sister worked up until her due date, so I'm sure I will too. I expect to have a c-section, as I did with my first birth. I expect to gain 60 pounds because my cousin did. I will return to my pre-pregnancy size and shape in 6 weeks because Sarah Jessica Parker did. Pregnancy is going to be a beautiful time in my life. Pregnancy is going to be a difficult and challenging time in my life. Pregnancy will be (fill in your expectation here).

At some point during your pregnancy you feel as if every expectation is in play. You don't know what to expect so you seek out advice and keep a very open mind. Eventually you begin to sort through your expectations, accepting some and rejecting others. You begin to expect more from others, to give yourself more care. You feel valued and important.

As with Rachel, the architect, your pregnancy expectations are really in sync with what you need and want, with how you perceive yourself and project yourself to others. As Rachel put it, "I wanted to show them you can react to situations with calm and grace. I needed to live by example. The more they fussed and fretted, the more I realized my pregnancy was mine. I could do it my way."

Unpregnancy is an opportunity to review your expectations, renegotiate them, and see their role in our everyday moods. Expectations have a way of controlling you and causing you stress. Our expectations are shaped by so many elements and they control our attitudes, moods, relationships, effectiveness, whom we trust, what kind of children we raise, and what kind of successes we have in nearly every endeavor. We have expectations of everyone in our network, from electrician to husband, mentor to child, teacher to friend.

Unpregnancy is a time when you can practically bottle your expectations and change your dose methodically to get the best mix of *what to expect when you're unexpecting*. If expectations could be bottled, they'd come with a warning label.

> **WARNING:** Expectations can control you. Expecting positive outcomes can result in a positive outlook, optimism, and enthusiasm. Expecting the worst can get you more of the same. Bad personal experiences can cause you to lower your expectations, but they can work in the reverse too. When administered with optimism, bad personal experiences can cause the patient to think optimistically: *I can do better than that*. So when altering the dose of expectation be careful to administer optimism in equal measure.

When your expectations are routinely at odds with reality and hostility results, maybe you're not getting the right information. Is someone tricking you? Hiding information from you? Not communicating? Or are they communicating and you're not taking in the information? Are you being too hard on yourself because of expectations you internalized from your parents long, long ago? Reconsider your expectations. Are they reasonable? Realistic? Communicated? And still ignored?

In pregnancy all your expectations naturally come under scrutiny and so become negotiable. This is a secret power, a secret gift given to you in pregnancy. It is a forgotten gift that you need to unwrap now during your Unpregnancy.

You can consciously choose to scrutinize the reigning assumptions in your life to change your moods and relationships, mitigate your stress, and get the help and love that you need. Changing your expectations can be very liberating! (Mood-altering.)

LABOR #20: INSPECT YOUR EXPECTATIONS

You need to work at changing your expectations, but also changing the effect your expectations are having on your moods. For a few days, keep your Morning Journal close at hand and look for expectations gone awry. Next time you're angry about something, write it down. See if you can take your angry reaction through the five steps below and figure out how to either change your expectation or get your expectation respected. Seek help and perspective from a friend—not necessarily to validate your expectation, but to see through it, as Dana did with her Unpregnancy group, below.

1.   **Write down the stress point.**

One mom, Dana, came back to our seminar one week and told everyone that she had written the following:

I'm mad because my sister Suzanne is late AGAIN.

Dana said it was her sister's fault that everything else in her day went poorly. It was ultimately Suzanne's fault that Dana didn't get her kids to bed on time and homework didn't get done and Dana couldn't get to sleep that night for a long time because she was still so angry at her sister.

2.   **Look for the underlying expectation.**

The moms commiserated with Dana. No one likes to be left waiting around and apparently Suzanne didn't even have kids, so what was her excuse? They could also tell that Dana had a higher-than-average need for timeliness. She was a working mom whose whole day relied on keeping to a rigorous schedule. Dana's schedule was tight some days, tighter on others. She didn't have the luxury of running late. She had begun to think that was true of everyone.

- Dana expected everyone to understand that if she got off-schedule by 15 minutes, she would spend the rest of the day making it up to people and be in a rotten mood by dinner.
- Dana's sister expected flexibility. After all, her life was pretty flexible. She didn't want to run on her sister's demanding schedule because it reminded her too much of their own mother's expectations.

3. Find a more realistic expectation.

Reasonable expectations are not the same as realistic expectations. To Dana, it was reasonable to expect her sister to be on time. Her kids managed to keep to a schedule, why couldn't a full-grown adult? One seminar mom pointed out a key question:

- *Why did Dana expect her sister to be on time when she never was?*
  Her expectation was reasonable (many people manage to show up on time), but not realistic (Dana's sister always ran late).

4. Work with the new, realistic expectation.

If it's not a realistic hope, give it up. Save your energy and do it differently next time by adjusting your "dose" of expectation.

- *What are Dana's options, given that her sister usually runs late?*
  She could start without her, tell her to come earlier than necessary, cue up a task to make the waiting time productive, talk to her sister about why it's important—critical in fact—for her to be on time or only see her sister under more relaxed circumstances, like on a weekend.

5. Try to negotiate a new set of expectations.

When Dana finally addressed how angry Suzanne's constant lateness made her, her sister was genuinely empathetic to how structured Dana's life had become, but she felt sure she couldn't live that way.

"Duh," thought Dana. "I've got a lot of responsibilities in a day and seeing you is one of my few pleasures. Then you ruin even that by being late."

"I can't just magically be on time because you need it," thought her sister. "Realistically, my life is demanding and out of my control. For my day to work, I need to remain flexible and open to schedule interruptions. Out of respect for your needs I can try harder, but I need some wiggle room, too."

I unrealistically expect to preside over a nice family dinner each night. I blame TV for that—*The Brady Bunch*, *The Cosby Show*, and the Camdens on *Seventh Heaven* all manage to make dinnertime look easy, delicious, and filled with togetherness. Cooking dinner, serving it, and then *not* sitting and enjoying it the way I envision creates stress for me nearly every night because it never goes the way I expect. Either I make a meal that no one eats because people aren't hungry or home at dinnertime, or I don't make a meal and then my family eats poorly. I see it as a personal failure. Resolving this stress with realistic data (and not a TV model) will take time, but for now I at least understand why I feel so unhappy every day at 6:00 p.m. I found the unrealistic expectation and can address it more directly.

We all have the "perfect moment" syndrome from television, movies, books, and stories. A good drama sets up all the expectations to go one way and despite every sign, the heroine gets a happy result. The heroine triumphs against all odds. Comedies set up every expectation of a reasonable result, then lead the audience to a ludicrous, silly result—but usually in the end, still a triumph. Romantic movies lead us to expect intimate and thoughtful gestures from our husbands that don't happen the way we've scripted them in our heads. Even if he were holding the script, he would probably resist delivering on unrealistic romantic expectations.

Big Changes, Great Expectations

What should we expect when we're *Un*expecting? Who will you turn to for advice or as a role model? How can you suddenly hope to achieve your goals, especially if you've failed in the past? How can you fill your Unpregnancy with delicious expectancy? How do you realistically expect that you'll prevail when those around you, even you yourself, can barely believe it will happen? If your Unpregnancy goals are linked to your mission, your natural ambitions, your greatness, then they're likely something you've been thinking about and *wanting* for a long time. You may have already tried to achieve your goal many times before. How do we achieve our great expectations?

Unpregnancy is the perfect opportunity for you to divorce yourself from old patterns and expectations, tired advice, and limiting attitudes. Your mother was never Unpregnant before. Your neighbor can't offer an opinion on how or what you should do. Your expectancy—your hopefulness—is strictly your own. Your expectation of success comes from within.

LABOR #21—BELIEVE IT

Think back to when you said to yourself, "I can't believe I'm going to have a baby" or "I can't believe I'm going to be a mother."

Remember how, even as you said this, you were smiling and you knew deep down inside: you believed. Even if it was hard to visualize, you knew your fate was promised. You were going to be a mother. Now, of course, you're a pro—you dress the part and act the part, even sometimes with other people's kids. No one would suspect this was once scary territory for you.

Complete this sentence with what you'll be once you achieve your three Unpregnancy goals for T1/Self, T2/Love and T3/Work.

1. I can't believe I'm going to be _____

2. I can't believe I'm going to be _____

3. I can't believe I'm going to be _____

Look at the three new roles you are going to assume and imagine that you are already that person, at ease with all three accomplishments. Skip past the giddy day you get "the call" and your dreams come true, and imagine that your accomplishments already determine how you act, who you tell people you are, how you dress, and what house you live in. Imagine you're an authority in your new area. You've been doing it for years and you've been asked to give a speech about how you got started and what advice you'd give others who are struggling to achieve the same goals.

Imagine what would be said about you in your introduction. Think about how you would be dressed. What would be your topic? Whom are you addressing? Who is cheering you on? What will your speech be about? Speak out now, addressing the imaginary audience, and in four to five minutes, tell the story of how you got where you are. (If you need help writing a speech, visit www.toastmasters.org.) Time your speech and record it. Listen to how you talk about yourself. Can you believe it now?

"Brand" New You

When it comes to drumming up support and selling your expectancy to others we can look to the master salespeople in our culture, the advertisers. Marketers and advertisers have championed what's called "branding." We all go to supermarkets and recognize brands, and when we pick one up—Tide or Diet Coke or Campbell's Soup—we know what to expect.

The first brands were simply someone's name and reputation—Henry J. Heinz's personal assurance that you could expect a good product, in 57 varieties. He stood in farmers' kitchens pedaling his pickles and horseradish sauces, building his brand and building expectations for the products' quality.

Like Henry Heinz, we all have personal brands—trademarks—whether we realize it or not. Your big changes and great expectations have to be communicated. They change who you are, and in essence, how you want to be treated or perceived. And what is a brand if it is not the essence of something, or in this case someone?

If like Henry Heinz your name is a brand, you can consider many of your conversations and actions advertising. You're not on TV, but people are watching you, looking up to you. The many ways you've changed add up to a new brand essence, and you have to let it show. Some of the changes you've made may not be popular, but sell the positive aspects with a smile.

You have to communicate and to tell people what to expect. The truth is, you do communicate your brand essence whether or not you're doing it well. You cannot not communicate. People expect certain things from you whether or not it's what you hope your brand communicates. You want to change their expectations, get them to accept and support your new brand essence.

Your big changes and great expectations may need to be packaged and sold. People are leery of change, so don't forget the WIIFM factor—What's in It for Me? If you want your friends and family to buy into unpopular changes, you may need to offer them something in return (the real-life equivalent of a coupon or free trial offer). Feel free to steal some of these ideas from advertisers. They could work in your home settings, too.

- **Try a Frequent Flier program**—Pay money or chits for what you would like others to do. This could be an allowance or an award program.

- **BOGO (Buy One Get One)**—Here are some examples: if your child tries the healthy dinner, you'll let him have the less healthy side dish, too. If your third grader reads to herself for 20 minutes, then you'll read to her for the next 20, until you can wean her off needing to be read to each night. If your teenager cleans her bathroom, you won't bug her about keeping her room clean.

- **Barter/Trade In**—You could barter a change with your friends or your husband. Examples: Your husband makes dinner on weekends, you make dinner on four weeknights and you order in every Friday. Swap weekends of babysitting so couples can take a weekend away together, alone. Two friends could make double Sunday dinners and give the extra to the other family for Monday.

- **Coupon**—Why not? Haven't your kids given you coupons for a "quiet cup of coffee" or "clean my room when asked" on Mother's Day? My kids get them from school, color them in and make them a gift. Ask your kids what they're worried about and give them a coupon to help alleviate their concerns. "This coupon, when presented promises *I'll drop you off at school and get donuts on the way; Or Make your favorite dinner; Or Take you to a movie.*"

Change can be hard for everyone, so you have to sell it. Your words and actions need to be proactive, positive, and firm, and they need to set up a new expectation, something that you and your friends and family *can believe in*.

LABOR #22—YOUR BRAND

Your brand is the essence of who you are. Think of who you are, in your community and in your family. How do you describe yourself? How do people perceive you? Remember that your name is your brand. What does your brand stand for? How well do you live up to peoples' expectations of you? How well do you advertise your brand essence—as new and improved? Are your family and friends responding well to your changes (both the popular and unpopular ones)?

To build expectancy for yourself and for those around you, you need to know your brand. The stakes are high because how you communicate your expectations and how you're perceived are essentially who you get to be. Do you buy in to the new you? Do your family and friends? For a personal brand, buy-in means freedom, power, and liberty to pursue happiness. Buy-in is belief in expectancy.

Let's look at your brand first in order to develop awareness of it. List 10 adjectives or nouns that describe you.

1. _____   6. _____

2. _____   7. _____

3. _____   8. _____

4. _____   9. _____

5. _____   10. _____

Without showing anyone else your list, ask several other people to describe you using 10 adjectives or nouns (positives only, please). Then do the same for those you've asked; they will be just as pleasantly surprised by how you describe them as you were about how they described you (it's like getting applause). This is by far the most popular and eye-opening exercise in any of my seminars. Because people are not sure how they are perceived and what attributes they project, it can be enormously helpful to become aware of your brand. You'll probably be pleasantly surprised.

❋ Compare your brand list with other people's lists.

❋ Is there a difference in how you think of yourself vs. how others perceive you?

❋ Look at your brand lists. Does your brand serve your core mission?

❋ Using your new brand awareness, think about who you are brand-wise, whether it serves your mission and whether you communicate your expectations well or not.

❋ Consider, too, how Unpregnancy might change your brand and your advertising. How will you act and speak differently?

Whether or not your Unpregnancy takes you into a business role, awareness of your brand, your essence, and what expectations your name drums up for the people you meet is very empowering and important experience.

What to Expect When You're Unexpecting

Unpregnancy gave me expectancy where previously I had none. It gave me back the idea of me as a person in the world, rather than me as a mom in the house. I understood—deeply—that if I could change my life, my expectations, my rights, and my personal space so dramatically during nine months to make a precious child, I could and would do the same for nine months to make my life more precious.

I began to scribble down my rules of Unpregnancy, since Unpregnancy is guided more by the spirit of pregnancy—awe, wonder, commitment, self-care—than by its physical guidelines. You don't have to quit drinking; you don't have morning sickness or backaches, so what are the expectations? I created a list of my expectancies.

LABOR # 23—BECOME AN EXPECTANT WOMAN

Create your own list of expectancies—your own rules of Unpregnancy. Use the alphabetical format if you want to or simply begin to write down rules and expectancies you have come to live by during your Unpregnancy. Although my expectancies are general, use this opportunity to customize your rules to your personal efforts. What do you expect?

I expect:

1. _____

2. _____

3. _____

4. _____

5. _____

6. _____

7. _____

8. _____

9. _____

10. _____

The Expectancies of Unpregnancy

All I want is all I've ever wanted—a rich, full life.

Beyond bottles, beyond babies is ME.

Comfort zone?!? Was pregnancy comfortable?

Deep thinking, deep desires, deep down commitment lead to exhilarating changes.

Everything you do is important.

Find your mission. Feel its life force.

Get full of yourself. The small wonder in your womb is YOU.

Hopefulness creates positivity, momentum, success and awe.

Insight: If you act in faith, your infrastructure appears.

Just nine months: long enough to change your life, but not too long to sustain focus.

Know thyself.

Love thyself.

Mother Nature smiles on your ambition. Make her proud.

No! is a powerfully positive statement. No, I will not fail.

Optimism is contagious.

Permission to put your feet up, granted.

Quell your critical inner voice.

Rest. Relax. Rejuvenate. Revive.

Shift your expectations. Shed the expectations of others.

Try. Fail. Try again.

Unscripted. Unexpected. Unpregnancy.

VIP—Very important priorities

Wonder at the world and its possibilities.

Xpress Yourself—your desires, your needs, your expectations.

Your authentic self is a unique work of art.

Zest and zeal are infectious!

Changing Your Life Forever

So many of us come to Unpregnancy expecting to change our lives forever. We're listening to a new biological clock—our own mortality. We feel the need to see our lives—our life expectancies—come true within our anticipated lifespan. The time to start is now.

Your life has limits and you begin to see those limits. They can be crushing or they can allow you to see specific possibilities. When you can see specifically what you want within the context of your life's limits it can be invigorating. Change brings new realities that can take you over the moon even if your current reality dictates that you'll need to have realistic expectations *en route*. Just as you need to take small steps and celebrate those small steps, you need to enjoy the moments, the process, and the interim achievements. You never know where your positive (realistic) expectations will take you. Attaining realistic, measurable goals could allow you to break through to a very different reality in your life (fame, fortune, a new love, an unexpected life gift). Should that be part of your Unpregnancy expectation? Why not? Go ahead, as long as you don't undervalue the more realistic steps it will take to get you headed in that direction. Enjoy the journey. If you're on the right road, it truly won't matter how far it takes you.

Make sure your expectations are realistic and make sure your new realities become your expectations. Allow reality to inform your enthusiasm, not to take it away.

Remember that even reasonable expectations may not be realistic. It is reasonable to want to relax on vacation, to expect to find peace of mind, but is it always realistic? It is reasonable to want to enjoy the holidays, to expect to have fun and to celebrate, but is it always realistic? Not all of our expectations can be met—it's just not realistic.

And yet experts agree that if you expect good things, you'll find good things; you are less likely to be deterred and disappointed even by a bad sequence of events. It's a silver lining approach that keeps each hope alive and gives expectations momentum even as reality intervenes.

LABOR #24: CREATE YOUR NEW REALITY

Get rid of old expectancies and create your new reality. As you make progress in your endeavors, find a way to shed your old skin like a snake. If you've lost a lot of weight, get rid of the clothes that don't fit anymore (donate them or give them away). In your new reality, you have no expectancy of ever needing them again. If you've given up a bad habit, get rid of its accoutrements. Throw away the lighters and ashtrays; give away the corkscrews and the stemware; get rid of the clutter from a left-behind reality.

Keep a single memento as your I A.M. Award (Labor #15). Celebrate your interim success with an ad hoc ceremony. Invite a family member to present the award and write an introduction about what they expected and what they saw happen (feel free to wear a tiara).

Removing a path back to your old self will do two things—change your own expectations for yourself and convince your friends and family that you're serious.

Take the time to go through closets, cabinets, drawers and desks to rid yourself of old expectancies. You will be amazed at how this physical break will free you emotionally.

napping is not a crime

JULIA'S JOURNAL

I was asleep. I admit it. My head was heavy and my legs were like logs. I looked in the mirror and saw my pinched, reddened face and I decided to lie down—just for a moment—but I couldn't help myself. Sleep came seductively. I'm getting up. Sleep pursued me. I'm just closing my eyes. Sleep entered my mind with a monotonous tone that grew in ever-widening circles. I knew I should focus; I thought to turn on the TV to distract myself or even better to serve as a reasonable cover story. Too late, I was dreaming.

I'm so ashamed. It's midday and I'm a full-grown woman! No one has to . . . zzzzzz . . . . In my dream, I'm not pregnant. I'm the opposite of pregnant. I'm energetic and unencumbered. I'm Unpregnant. Hmmm, I think, wouldn't that be nice for a change? To be Unpregnant. No more wondering if I really look like that from behind. No more having to pee in the middle of every movie, in the middle of everything. No more tears at Kodak commercials or hand-me-down maternity clothes. Why don't they tell you about hemorrhoids? I guess they do, but who knew? Everyone wants to touch you. I'm tired of body attention instead of real attention. In this dream, I realize that a roomful of loving, anticipatory faces are turned toward me.

And the winner is . . . Julia Roberts! I'm called to the front of the room in my vintage Valentino designer dress. I look fabulous (and not pregnant at all). Beautiful people applaud. There's the OTHER Julia Roberts. Omigod, is this HER award? Did they mean Julia Roberts, HER? I approach the podium from stage left and she approaches from stage right. We lock eyes across the proscenium. WE'RE WEARING THE SAME DRESS! Why am I dreaming myself in the same black and white dress she wore to the Oscars for Erin Brokovich? Can't I just rewrite, rethink, re-dream? Ugh. We are both mortified, but certainly everyone will consider ME the imposter. I'm nervous and hot under the lights. I feel a little trickle of sweat trying to obey gravity and run down my cheek. I brush my face and tears well up in my eyes. Why is Julia Roberts here? (Why am I the imposter in my own dream?)

I brush my cheek again—what is that? A fly? It's disrupting my dream. I try to wave it away again, but it is persistent. I look over at Julia Roberts and try to summon what dignity I can to face this challenge. What do I do? They're going to think I'm the crasher. I look to the presenter for some reassurance. (That fly again!) It's poking me in the ribs and shaking my shoulders. What's with this fly? I take a last look at the presenter at the podium, who is holding a statuette for me. I can't stay in this dream and accept this award. I'm awake. Abruptly, I'm in my own living room, lolling on the couch. The fly begins to feel more like a gruff human hand. My eyes open and . . . I'm busted.

The Nap Police! What was I thinking? Had I left the doors open? Did a neighbor spy me through the window? I glanced up at the open blind and felt regret spread in the pit of my stomach. My mind was racing: EVERYONE IS GOING TO KNOW THEY'RE ARRESTING ME. THEY'RE GOING TO CALL MY HUSBAND AT WORK TO COME BAIL ME OUT! WHAT WILL MY PARENTS THINK? THE KIDS WILL BE TEASED AT SCHOOL. But then the Nap Police see that I'm pregnant. They apologize and leave.

Napping is not a crime when you're pregnant (or Unpregnant).

Without a doubt, we live in a " you-snooze-you-lose" society. Lollygagging is not allowed. But who enforces that standard? People who want you to work hard and not think too much about your potential outside of your job or your responsibilities. It's an attitude we support when we need to repress ideas and keep our noses to the grindstone. Only salespeople, athletes, supermodels and actors need to be consistently competitive. It's an idea we buy into as a career builder because it makes our jobs seem more important and our role in a big company feel grander. It's one way to convince ourselves that the pace, the expectations, the pressure, and the unpleasant criticism are all worth it and for our own good.

Even in the midst of your success, your competitive vigilance, your eyes-on-the-prize attitude, your Sisyphean task, you may need a nap. You may need a pause. Pregnancy may be the last time you had a pause or a distraction, a realignment of your priorities, values, and expectations. Attitudinally, your Unpregnancy may be like waking up from a nap refreshed, with a new vision and renewed momentum. Sometimes I judge my worth by how much

I manage to do in a day. I have a hard time relaxing and sleeping at night if I feel I didn't achieve a lot in any given day. Some nights, I hold myself to a ridiculous standard. So how do I square an afternoon nap with my internal Napping Police? On any day when I feel I actually need a nap or a break of some sort, I schedule it. Then checking it off my To Do list makes it a good thing, an accomplishment. By some accounts 50 percent of Americans are sleep-deprived. I'm simply doing my part to end this epidemic.

Caught napping implies so much more than just catching 40 winks. *Caught napping* is intended to make you feel selfish, like you've stolen something, cheated someone, or napped on your watch. Power-napping is a phrase that has been created to bring napping out of the closet and ally it with its potential benefit. According to William Anthony in *The Art of Napping*, great nappers include JFK, Winston Churchill, Thomas Edison, Jim Lehrer, Leonardo DaVinci, and Bill Clinton.

Any guilty pleasure can be put into perspective. I'm forced to admit that I play Solitaire on my computer when I should be working. So call the Solitaire police. Once a client " caught" me playing Solitaire in their offices when I was charging an exorbitant hourly rate. His reaction? *We're all shakin' in our boots about this presentation and she knows she has the concept nailed. She's in there playing Solitaire!* In my defense, I was waiting for their feedback on a completed proposal.

We all need an opportunity to rest, to take a deserved break or a loving pause. It's not a waste of time because it is positively approached, lovingly given, and accepted by you. We all need a weird and wakeful dream that gives us the right to a nap.

LABOR #25—GUILTY PLEASURES

Make a list of five guilty pleasures:

1. _____

2. _____

3. _____

4. _____

5. _____

Are any of them addictive? Do you feel guilty enjoying them in an appropriate way, as a brief respite from your task? Which is the real problem in accomplishing your task—the guilt or the pleasure? Are there some indulgences (like watching TV?) that you could enjoy more if you set limits or guidelines?

Permission to Put Your Feet Up

As you sit on a balcony overlooking the water, the waiter brings you an iced drink while another handsome devil gives you a foot massage. You take a multivitamin, request another day off, and contemplate a swim later in the afternoon. Sound too good to be true? Successful people can manage this kind of luxury, right? Why is that? Is it their success that affords them luxury or are they successful because they value themselves enough to take good care of themselves and reward themselves *on a regular basis?* People who treat themselves with respect earn respect from others, and people who enforce personal limits have power. Only martyrs and saints work tirelessly without reward. You don't have to give up the goal to nab a nap. If you're feeling resentful, overworked, and underappreciated, you're probably all of those things.

When you were pregnant, you let people wait on you or you at least felt deserving even if you eschewed their help. Even if you've never asked for or received a massage from your partner at any other time in your marriage, you were probably offered one during pregnancy (or at least you had a reasonable, if not realistic expectation of one).

What about getting your rest, eating right, and giving your brain a vacation? You gave yourself those gifts, right? Caring for yourself is part of what makes pregnancy so positive. You're not on a diet, you're feeding yourself and your baby. You're not being lazy, you're resting. Each step you take to care for yourself increases your self-esteem, your worth and your sense of achievement and value.

Your Unpregnancy is a time to care for yourself, to indulge yourself, to insist on time off to refuel away from the stress of your life. Dump multitasking and embrace multishirking! (How many petty expectations can you shirk at one time?)

Not only does shirking give you more self-value, it reduces your everyday clutter and allows you a chance to be in touch with yourself and have greater life satisfaction.

LABOR #26: MOTHER YOURSELF

Schedule an appointment to care for your self or indulge a self-nurturing whim. Take one of my ideas or go back to your Feel Wonderful list (Labor #14).

- **Get a manicure and pedicure.**
- **Schedule a massage or walk in for a 10-minute shoulder and neck rub.**
- **Visit Unpregnancy.com for a friendly visit with other moms.**
- **Take yourself out for an outrageous and delicious salad.**
- **Take a hot bath with candles.**
- **Call in " well" at work—and take the day off.**
- **Make a wish on a star or toss a coin in a fountain.**
- **Make jam with seasonal fruit.**
- **Visit PositivePause.com.**
- **Build a fire in your indoor/outdoor fireplace.**
- **Teach your spouse or friend a beloved card game.**
- **Visit a museum.**
- **Bet a prepared dinner for two that you can win a friendly card game, board game or word game.**
- **Go canoeing.**
- **Create a beaded necklace.**
- **Book a weekend getaway, alone, or with your husband or a friend.**

- Enjoy getting lost while driving, cycling or walking in the woods.
- Invite a friend or group of friends for a fireside tea in winter or a picnic lunch at a waterfall in spring or summer.
- Read Emily Dickinson or Shel Silverstein's *Where the Sidewalk Ends* or Stacey Handler's *The Body Burden*—there are laughs, insights, and pleasure in poetry. Write your own.
- Rediscover the passionate voices of singers like Ella Fitzgerald, Betty Carter, Edith Piaf, or Nina Simone.

The Pregnant Pause

As a writer, I gestate. I think and I procrastinate. Sometimes I eat, sometimes I rearrange the playroom or call my sister or run to Target on an urgent mission. Procrastination is part of my process. If I beat myself up in any one of these significant phases of creation, I've disturbed the process. The difference between positive procrastination and plain escapism is in how I prepare for the digression.

By definition the pregnant pause is weighty, significant, and anticipatory. In a staged performance, it's the brief eternity between a loaded question and a long-awaited response. It is a true pause—a break in the action—when focus is demanded and relinquished willingly. It is engagement. You are open to ideas and oddly pregnable. You're letting thoughts in even as you engage in mindless physical activity.

This is Gestation.

Why take the pregnant pause? Because process is sometimes overlooked and undervalued. Without process we'd have no product. (Without ants we'd have no peonies.) We love the moment that the idea blooms, but the work itself is a lot less glamorous. Before-and-after pictures fascinate us, because we can't believe that these two very different-looking people can be one in the same. We flit from one photo to the other, entranced, and merrily overlook the months of hard work it took to transform in such a dramatic way.

Process, like pregnancy, is forgotten once it is lived through. Just as we love the moment the butterfly emerges from its chrysalis but have no interest in its time in the cocoon, we favor achievement and dismiss process. We need the pregnant pause to process our feelings about what we are undertaking in

Unpregnancy. When I sit down to write, I may reach a point at which no new idea comes. So I pause. Still no idea? I pause longer. I might do a little task, like making the bed or pouring coffee. I might still come up dry and leave the house (or switch on the TV). Now it is a question of integrity. Am I still processing? Is it true ambivalence or even writer's block or am I simply procrastinating? Only I can answer that. If I remain upbeat about the digression, I remain open to thoughts bubbling up and ideas taking form. If I feel guilty about the delay, I close my fortress doors and block the productivity of my pregnant pause. Everyone knows you get your best ideas in the shower and that's because in the shower you're engaging in a positive, self-caring digression.

If you've been trying to untie a knot and worked at it until you seem to have only made it worse, isn't it best to put it aside for now? In the time away from the knot, it will not change; its tightness will not relax, but you just might, and then you can bring yourself back to the task with a new approach or energy.

If you're indulging in a pregnant pause, it will be fruitful, weighty and significant. Just remember that the knot is still there, waiting, unchanged. The dramatic question hangs in the air and the audience is still rapt. Allow yourself time to gestate and then act. Return to the task; relieve the tension. End the suspense for yourself and your audience. You might work at the knot, picking it up several times in vain—and then all of a sudden and without fanfare, the knot unravels. Unpredictably, satisfyingly, a quiet drama unfolds in your hands. The process may not be smooth and it may be different for each person, but you need to discover yours and trust it to take you away from the central task and back again with vision and purpose. Self-exploration and *action* combine to create the you that you are seeking.

LABOR #27: PREGNANT QUESTIONS

If you feel guilty about a pregnant pause, ask yourself:

* **Am I processing?**
* **Am I avoiding?**
* **Am I relaxed and open to ideas?**
* **Am I stressed and feeling escapist?**
* **Is guilt closing down my process?**
* **Has my process been fruitful in the past?**
* **Do I fear failure in this endeavor?**
* **Do I fear success?**
* **Am I at a standstill and don't know how to proceed?**
* **Do I feel I need help and hesitate to ask?**
* **Can I solve the problem in my head or do I need to physically reapproach the problem?**

Dream or Drain

Processing and procrastination are certainly not the superheroes of most motivational methods. So much of our motivational jargon and expectation comes from the sports and corporate worlds, where people are paid by the hour, ranked competitively, and evaluated numerically, by percent of sales increase, profits earned, or points scored.

Unpregnancy takes its roots from pregnancy and it can teach us that waiting and creative procrastinating are part of the process that can help us birth our newborn selves. Your evolving self cannot be numerically defined. Once you've validated your process and know from personal experience that it will work, then you need to trust it, even if it includes socially scorned work methods like napping, talking on the phone, or making a beautiful dinner for two.

And what if you delay beginning your project indefinitely? What if other priorities continue to call you away from your dream goals? What if your busyness springs from other people's needs and others' vision for how to use your time?

How do you make your life yours again? How do you put yourself at the top of your priority list? How do you get the bedroom closets, the unfinished basement, and the financial paper-pushing out of your psyche and return to the musing and gestating that will bring you back to your mission?

Of the things you can't get to, dreams are what you *want* to do and can't get to, and drains are what you *don't* want to do and therefore can't get to. Drains could be literally allowing your dreams to slip away. Before you can take on the positive dream-building, you might need to stop up the drain. It's a "Catch-22"—are you spinning your wheels on small tasks to avoid confronting a scary dream? Or are you pursuing a dream only to be held back by unfinished business? If you have begun your dream effort in earnest only to find your positive energy sapped by an eyesore or an organizational black hole, schedule time to fix it.

I'll commit a bit of ad-napping and use Nike's tagline: *Just do it.* Drains suck, *literally*. They sap your energy, steal your focus, and deplete your enthusiasm. We return to the question of integrity—be honest with yourself. Is this task dragging you down or are you just focusing on it to avoid your true mission? Are you settling for a happy, accomplished, busy feeling instead of pursuing the harder tasks? Consider ways to divide your drain-work into a pregnant pause, in small increments. Do not begin a draining project unless you give yourself the time and opportunity to finish it, because that will simply leave you feeling even more unsettled. If you decide this task must happen before anything else, do it and do it well. Let yourself feel the satisfaction and then get back to your core mission.

LABOR #28: DRAINING EXPERIENCE

What's draining your energy? List five things that drag you down.

1. _____

2. _____

3. _____

4. _____

5. _____

Now circle the one-time projects that could be accomplished in a day or less. Cross out the tasks that are ongoing drains in your life (like doing laundry).

Lighten your Load by Enlisting Help

Saint Julia wouldn't complain about laundry or preparing dinner on week-nights. But *I* do. I am not a complainer unless I know that a complaint will be effective. I prefer to complain with a plan. I happen to be truly lucky in that I have already been effectively relieved of so many tasks that would drain my energy. My husband does laundry. I haven't vacuumed in decades (I have a cleaning lady) and up until this year a babysitter fed the kids each night. At various times in my life, I have had a personal assistant and a computer SWAT team to swoop in and rescue my failing network. How do I manage? There are ways to barter, swap and pay in kind to get many of your needs met. It's my life and I don't want to spend it vacuuming! If it's an emotional drain on your energy, find a way to put it aside.

Look at the list above of what's draining your energy. Let's try to get them out of your life. Look at the tasks you circled, the one-time projects. Break down those tasks into smaller, specifically defined jobs. Once you've clearly broken up the job into parts, you can consider which parts you can share with someone else and which only you can do. You can group the tasks in an efficient man-ner—out-of the-house errands, dirty work, phoning or thinking/researching/planning. Furthermore, once you've broken these tasks down into two-hour tasks, you'll find them more bearable, even if you don't enlist help.

If a job is unbearable for emotional reasons (like emptying a house after a divorce or death) seek help from a friend or family member.

JOB: CLEAN OUT MY CLOSET

2-hour task: Measure closet; research closet fittings/options; consider refitting with new hanging rods/upper and lower/front and back? List what options would fit in my closet.

2-hour task: Remove all clothes, shoes, etc. Vacuum and wipe down closet walls, floors and ceiling. Sort clothes into yes/no/maybe piles; make decision about closet organizers based on clothing/organizational needs.

2-hour task: Try on/consider "maybe" clothes. Check all "yes" and "maybe" clothes for stains, rips, suitability in your lifestyle (here's where a friend's eye could really help). Donate "no" clothes; purchase closet org pieces and hardware while out.

2-hour task: Refit new closet rods, storage cubes, drawers, if desired; rehang desired clothes by seasonality (front/back?) and type (high/low rods); shirts, skirts, dresses, suits, pants.

JOB #1

2-hour task:

2-hour task:

2-hour task:

2-hour task:

2-hour task:

JOB #2

2-hour task:

_____

_____

_____

2-hour task:

_____

_____

_____

2-hour task:

_____

_____

_____

2-hour task:

_____

_____

_____

2-hour task:

_____

_____

_____

JOB #3

2-hour task:

_____

_____

_____

_____

2-hour task:

_____

_____

_____

2-hour task:

_____

_____

_____

_____

2-hour task:

_____

_____

_____

2-hour task:

_____

_____

_____

_____

Shower the People You Love with Love

Time for an Unpregnancy shower! You may know other Unpregnant women or simply friends trying to make their lives work. Ask them over for an Unpregnancy shower.

Host an Unpregnancy shower with your other Unpregnant or sympathetic friends and bring the lists above as your gift registry. Invite your guests to do the same. You can agree as a group on how many two-hour tasks you're willing to commit to (whatever you agree to give, you'll get back). Now write your tasks on slips of paper and let the guests circulate and sign up for whom they'll help on which projects. You will be gifting someone else with your time as well. You will help someone through a job they have dreaded— a great gift to give a friend—and you will have help and company when you undertake your least favorite job.

Once someone has registered for one or two of your gifts, they'll seek you out to arrange a convenient time. It will be your obligation to be home, prepared to begin the job at the start time and with the appropriate materials. Your Unpregnant friend will help you stop up that energy drain. Chances are your friend will have a less encumbered approach to your problems and will be very effective in cutting the task down to size. If your friend gets in the spirit of things and stays and helps an extra two hours, make sure you make it clear that she can count on you for an extra two-hour gift of your time for an onerous task in her life.

When gifting your time, try to choose tasks where you have a gift, experience or a talent, such as organizing, painting, helping someone with wardrobe decisions, tax/financial organization, or technology savvy. The gift will be of greater value and a greater pleasure for both of you.

Once everyone has gifted the pre-agreed number of tasks, spend some time brainstorming ways to alleviate each other's remaining energy drains. Don't be shy about asking for solutions for the kinds of drains everyone has to endure—like paying bills. There are ways around every task and ways to simplify every job. We don't normally ask our friends for help with finding ways to cook dinner or how to keep ants out of the pet food or other emotionally draining mundane tasks in our lives. But it is worth the effort if that task represents an emotional drain for you.

I've gotten great ideas from other women about how to plug the drains. Some of the free solutions I've used: I offered an extra room in my house for the summer to a college intern via an ad in the school newspaper. In exchange for the room, she paid me with 15 hours per week of clerical/organizing help. I've unearthed a talented *eighth-grader* to come help me with my computer woes when regular technicians couldn't be bothered (even at their sky-high hourly rates). I've bartered babysitting with another mother of an infant to give us both time to locate freelance work. I set up a backyard summer camp for my son and four friends. Each of the five moms committed to one weekday to host the five boys. For one day's efforts, I established four free days a week for myself. There's a reason potluck suppers are enjoying a comeback. It's fun to handle the work in a social, creative way.

You can always send your laundry out—it may not seem worth it, but have you actually checked how much it would cost? You can hire a personal chef (*dream on)* or consider the true cost-to-value ratio of purchasing more prepared entrees or cooking on Sundays for the entire week. Or learn a few time-savings tricks. Cook once, eat twice. Grill extra chicken breasts for dinner and use the excess in a chicken salad for lunches. Create a lunch rotation with two or three friends at work. You pack for three people once a week and enjoy healthy, inexpensive lunches all week. Then the four of you have Fridays off. Swap a casserole/stew/soup with a neighbor on a weekly basis. It is just as easy to make a double batch and delightful to eat something (*any-thing)* you didn't personally have to make.

Years ago, we hosted a Murder Mystery party for my daughter's twelfth birthday. We wanted to send out an invitation that said something like "Murder at _____ Mansion." We needed a name for the fictional mansion—our house. Of course we wanted an appropriately pretentious name for our house, reminiscent of British aristocracy. We dubbed our house "Lollalot Manor." Everyone knows we love to loll around.

I have found my calling, and it is *lolling.*

t2/checkup

In the second trimester, you shared your joy. How do you feel? How is your home life improved? Are you forming more or better friendships? Have you been surprised by the amount of help available to you when you ask?

Place a checkmark by all the steps you have been taking to ensure a positive outcome of your Unpregnancy Love goal.

- ○ Just be.
- ○ Seek the help of friends and family.
- ○ Find a way to accept the wait or delay in your progress.
- ○ Eliminate false labor.
- ○ Change your expectations and shed others' expectations of you.
- ○ Mother yourself and take a day off.
- ○ Host an Unpregnancy shower or barter help with a friend.

Are you maintaining your contact with the Unpregnancy community?

- ○ Use the e-tools on www.unpregnancy.com.
- ○ Keep in touch with your midwife and/or Unpregnancy group.
- ○ Keep your Morning Journal four to seven days a week.
- ○ Keep a journal of tasks you need to reach your goal (e.g., a food diary).
- ○ Track the measurable changes on a daily or weekly basis.

PART THREE:

you're showing

third trimester—work

Six months into your new undertaking you'll be "showing." People will notice you're having too much fun, looking too good for your age. Your newfound confidence, happiness, and higher expectations have had a positive impact on you that everyone can see. Believe me, strangers will smile at you. It's time to take on the world.

For Unpregnancy to have the transformational effect that you hope for, third trimester goals should be awe-inspiring. Ask yourself, *Can I do it?*, and make sure your goals are awesome, but achievable. Do not sell yourself short. If you have a strong desire but you have no idea how you can achieve it, don't give up. Even if your goal is too ambitious for the remaining three-month period, find a way to make a valid and committed start during the last trimester. (Like a newborn, just a start, but a darn good one.) Get inspired! Talk to the friends and family you've been reconnecting with—it's amazing how much information you'll have access to if you just ask. (Nobody has a baby by herself, right?)

By the third trimester, you've found your center and increased your love and support at home. You've managed to eliminate annoying obligations and phony commitments so you're ready to commit to what's really important *to you*. In this trimester, you will begin to find opportunities to grow into the career and community roles you aspire to.

Career Goals

Most of us are accustomed to goals relating to work. If we have goal aversion, it's because most of our goals were created and enforced in the workplace by some boss. Remember, these are *your* goals for the workplace, not your boss's.

I can clearly recall a conversation with a boss, early in my career, when I was accused of not being a team player. I reminded him that he was the team and I was the player. The only way to get teamwork is to keep the players happy. Don't forget to take a step back and make sure that what you're working so hard for is what *you* want. Does it fit into your Unpregnancy mission? Is your career taking you where you want to go? Is this a good time to give some serious thought to researching opportunities or avenues you could pursue with some of your established skills and talents? Your Unpregnancy career goal may have absolutely nothing to do with your current job. You may love your job, your boss, and your career. Bravo! That makes you an authority and a potential mentor; perhaps when it comes to your third trimester, all you need to do is find a rewarding way to give back or keep up your good work and find another creative or rewarding avenue for your work goal. You might consider a community goal.

You may have to keep your job—whether you like it or not—in order to pay bills, even if a little soul searching illustrates a deep-seated need to change careers. How you manage that has to do with how much you need an ongoing and reliable income. But if your Unpregnancy reveals a mandate to change your career you can at least construct the path to change.

If you haven't yet, be sure to take a personality test that will help you understand your niche, your unique talents, and what you can offer an employer. (There are links to personality tests at www.unpregnancy.com) One long-revered test is the Myers-Briggs personality test. You answer many, many questions and arrive at an understanding of yourself that is uncanny. By the time you're done scoring the test, you fit into one of 16 personality types. I was bowled over by the test results, but what floored me wasn't the test's ability to take the vast amounts of information I had just provided about myself and condense it into a powerfully good description of me. After all, that is just data in/data out. What impressed me is that even as I read an insightful, enlightening description of me, it dawned on me that the description of me was *not* a description of everyone else. What I have to offer is available in only one out of 16 personalities—that's just 6.25 percent of humans. I'm rare, just as you are. I'm hard to find, if what you need is someone like me. So if I insist on finding work and surroundings that demand something that is uniquely me, my value will be very high indeed.

If you're just reentering the workforce, you have an excellent opportunity to get it right the first time. Make sure your moneymaking choices feed your soul, not just your family's hungry mouths. Visit www.unpregnancy.com for links to career resources. Follow your bliss and the money will follow.

Labor—Career

Ask yourself the following questions:

1. Who are you?

Take a Myers–Briggs personality test and use the description that creates for you. Once you know yourself better, in comparison to everyone else in the world, you can present your strengths as unique and valuable. What you take for granted—your organization, your ideas, your sense of humor, your outgoing personality—others are seeking. You only have to be able to articulate who you are and what you have to offer. People who value that personality type will find you—and cherish you.

2. What do you want?

Make a list of what you're looking for and cannot, will not, live without in a perfect job (your mission statement will clarify this answer for you). Does it have to be flexible? Do you require structure, benefits, creative freedom, guidance?

3. Where is the action?

What's going on in your chosen industry? Do some Internet research or ask people in the field. Begin reading the trades and trade-specific classified ads. What are the trends? What is growing? What is shrinking? Where are opportunities in the marketplace? Find areas that are currently growing and people who are leading the industry forward.

4. When will you succeed?

People succeed when they understand how their skill sets match existing jobs in the marketplace and when they hear about the job early in the process. How could you begin from where you are and land an existing job? Do you understand what various job titles entail? Are you aiming too high or too low? Could you get certified or take a seminar for a portion of the new job? Do you need accreditation from an outside source? Even long after school, you could benefit from a recommendation letter written by a friend in that field, someone to assure potential employers that you can make the leap into the new career area.

5. Why would a VIP speak to you?

Apparently, through a network of friends, we can all access Oprah via Kevin Bacon—it's a matter of just six degrees of separation. Start a list of whom you need to get to. You can find their names in trade magazines or by asking people on the phone. Magazines list their staff on the masthead and most corporations' personnel can be found on their website or by using Hoover's business listings. Once you know who you want to get to, be on the lookout for friends and acquaintances who might know someone who knows someone. Even family members don't necessarily volunteer their contacts, not because they're unwilling, but because they may not think of it *unless you ask*.

COMMUNITY GOALS

My Unpregnancy took an unexpected turn toward community in my third trimester. I had always been very career oriented in my ambitions. I had income goals, time-use goals, and very high expectations for my career, so goal setting was hardly unknown to me. During the process of Unpregnancy, I found that those goals were habitual. I hadn't rethought those habits since I began working, when all my ambition and effort went into building a career and salary. I ended up with a pretty successful career that I did not enjoy. I was stuck with it because my family needed the income and I wasn't sure how to change careers. Where I had once been gung-ho, now I was just a "ho." Doing the job was still an obligation, but giving up the career building gave me back time, energy, and focus.

I took on a community goal, one I would never have committed to when my career was paramount. The realization that my career was not building toward something I truly wanted freed me up. I put my energy and commitment into helping my good friend get a community pool built in our town. In leadership roles, we partnered to begin the project and pushed it into reality. We each committed more than 15 hours a week to this project in our small town. It took nearly three years, but my personal commitment to see it through—to make it my own mission—began with my first Unpregnancy. We ran publicity campaigns, organized membership drives, chaired events, and petitioned the town council for a new pool utility. Simply put, getting the community pool built became one of the greatest achievements of our lives.

LABOR—COMMUNITY

Revisit your giving policy that you wrote in Lesson #2. Have you limited your giving to causes and endeavors that fit your policy? Are you building a specific giving expertise? The giving options are myriad: food management and events, medical fundraising, caregiving, teaching, or any other giving mission that you really care to support.

You might find that you have a passion or unusual ability to help a certain type of person (adolescents, toddlers, homeless people, the elderly, teachers) or those with a specific need (estate planning, business planning, marketing, design, organizing). Finding your path back to paid work may come through passionate giving. You may find that your desired professional experience can be achieved and references earned through volunteer stints.

One Unpregnancy mom, Heidi, worked in the marketing field where she made good money and was lucky to have established herself in a part-time role. She felt guilty about not appreciating her good fortune, so she fulfilled her passion as a board member for a not-for-profit corporation where she could see that her own work made such a difference to so many kids. She volunteered more hours than she worked because she loved the organization. Not surprisingly, she managed to transfer her professional skills to a nonprofit service agency where she helps other agencies develop the materials they need to reach audiences and educate beneficiaries about diseases and programs. She is now in a paid position and very happy about how her work contributes to the world at large.

GOAL WISE

You're headed into your last trimester and this is your time. You're beginning to pursue what is hopefully a lifelong ambition. Take another minute to check your commitment to your goal. Awaken your past ambitions.

List five dream careers or ambitions of yesteryear

1. _____

2. _____

3. _____

4. _____

5. _____

List five things in your world you wish someone would change.

1. _____

2. _____

3. _____

4. _____

5. _____

Is there any correlation between your long-lost ambitions and the changes you'd like to see implemented? Circle the two that have a connection. Can this be your calling?

❋   **Are you still committed to the T3 goal you made six months ago?**

❋   **Is there an ambition above that still really tugs at you, even if it is a wild dream, like becoming an astronaut? Don't worry right now about any limitations, such as age, money, or opportunity. As long as you'll enjoy the journey, the destination can be far, far away.**

❋   **Frame your T3/Work goal in positive language and underline the mantra. Begin to say it at least twice a day for the next 21 days.**

❖ Have you looked into or begun to learn what you'll need to know to get started? Identify seminars, people to talk to, trade magazines to begin reading, etc.

❖ Have you identified or contacted a potential mentor? Someone you can ask to lunch in order to pick his or her brain?

❖ Are you ready to take steps to create pressure and push yourself out into the big world?

❖ Can you see your goals coming to pass?

❖ Are you nervous, excited, ready?

is mother nature kidding me?

Pregnancy and birth are perfectly natural, of course. Women have been giving birth since the dawn of mankind. Birth may not come quite as naturally as say, brushing your teeth, though that practice has only been around for a few hundred years. Women give birth every single day. Sure, childbirth is natural, but is it normal? Not a chance. When I was pregnant, my Grandma Dot made a long distance telephone call (a rare indulgence for her) to tell me, *You keep doing whatever you usually do. Carrying a child is not an illness.* Pregnancy is a normal part of a woman's life and yet we'd all agree it is life-altering.

And it is life-altering even before the child arrives and actually alters our lives. The mere fact of the impending birth and the steps you take to prepare for the baby give your life new meaning, purpose, ambition, hope, and expectation. You had a new normal and what came naturally to you was different, forever.

You got a good dose of maternal instinct, the deep-seated desire to nurture and invest in the young, the love and attachment that transform women at birth. It is true that when women give birth, they are transformed in ways too numerous and subtle to yet fully understand, according to Sarah Blaffer Hrdy in *Mother Nature—Maternal Instincts and How They Shape the Human Species*. Did you know, for instance, that the birth process enhances a woman's sense of hearing and smell for the rest of her life? (The growth of eyes-in-the-back-of-your-head is not scientifically supported.)

Hrdy's life work has entailed an analysis of maternal instinct in primates (including humans) over the past million years and a rethinking of mothers' natural roles and contributions to the evolution of the species. Charles Darwin, who lived during the Victorian era, was the first to introduce the notion of maternal instinct as part of his theory of evolution. The Victorians were prudes who repressed sexuality on every level. In polite company, chair legs were referred to as "limbs" and chicken breasts as "white meat" so as not to make a proper lady blush. The Victorians interpreted Darwin's findings about maternal instinct to rationalize their own prudish sense of males and females. What they found remarkable was the incredible self-sacrifice of mothers in nature—birds who would die defending their young, a spider who overeats after giving birth so her young can eat her and thrive.

Mothers were imbued with maternity, selflessness, passivity and a nurturing instinct by their very nature. And as Victorians saw it, whatever was applicable to mothers was the same for all women, since it was simply assumed that all women certainly would become mothers if they could. The other fact of nature that the Victorians espoused was the obvious dependency of women on men; since primates birthed complex, long-dependent children, it was clear that mothers could not survive without help during a child's infancy. As Darwin pointed out, a woman could not earn a living (gather food, ward off predators, keep shelter) while she nursed an infant. Victorians surmised that women were therefore inherently weaker—i.e., in need of protection, dependent, gentle, and submissive. They were considered very much like the children their instincts led them to care for.

Because motherhood was sanctified in the Victorian era, the Victorians failed to take note of the darker side of maternal instinct, a side considered immoral, unfeminine, and therefore not maternal. As Darwin observed, a primate mother (across species, across thousands of years) will go to great lengths to keep her infants alive and allow them to thrive. She has a vested interest not in the quantity of children born, but in the quality of the child and its life, so she attaches to her infant for life in order to bring him to maturity and see him reproduce. It is *in her nature* to choose with whom she will reproduce and under which circumstances she'll give birth. Mother Nature gave females many natural forms of birth control:

- Natural ways to attract and choose her most supportive mate and repel nonsupportive ones.
- Natural ways to space out births—menstruation cycles instead of "heats" and nursing interludes that act as a natural birth control.
- Natural ways to prevent unviable, unsupportable births—life-threatening stress or hunger can cause miscarriages; presence of disease or deformity can cause stillborn births; and deformed infants do not typically survive in the wild.
- Natural ways to not invest in an infant she cannot support. A primate mother will abandon or sometimes kill her infant (or allow it to be killed) if the father has been killed or defeated. She can't support it, so

she instinctively acts to ready herself for a new pregnancy in the hope that it would come under more auspicious circumstances.

In order to bring more healthy and strong offspring to maturity, maternal instinct also imbues mothers with ambition. Post-nursing phase, she works to improve her offspring's circumstances, creating a social network to help protect and support her. She rises in the ranks of her group through competition with other females. She moves her shelter closer to the protection of group males in order to avoid predators. (Ambition is not widely reported as part of maternal instinct, because Victorians didn't approve of this natural behavior.)

Mother Nature gives women *ambition*. It is the natural instinct of mothers. Depending on where you are on the mothering continuum, you may be surprised by this information—or perhaps not. When you're alone with an infant or toddler or both all day, it's hard to think of yourself as ambitious. At most, you might remember your ambitions and resent not being able to get back to them.

Do you consider yourself ambitious? Does that adjective sit well with you? (If not, blame the Victorians.) Traditionally, women value not their own careers per se, but the beneficiaries of that career—their kids, patients, constituents, etc. Women are more comfortable with lifelong "dreams" rather than "ambitions." To put it mildly, ambition is often regarded as unfeminine and yet your femininity is beyond question. You are a mother: *Been there. Done that.*

I asked a mother if she considered herself ambitious. She said that she was not, but then reflected for a moment and replied, "I used to be." She continued, "I consider myself to be an ambitious person, but what I apply my ambition to now is very different from when I was in my twenties. I still think I might get back to my early ambitions, but I'm okay with it if I don't. You have to relinquish some ambitions when you are raising kids."

Are mothers naturally ambitious? Are we afraid to compete with men or are we instinctively programmed not to? Is ambition different for us before and after our children's births? Hrdy documents the ways in which birth transforms us, and our own experiences validate this fact: when you were pregnant, you felt ambitious and excited in a new way and you were rewarded and recognized for your accomplishment.

But how your life would unfold was less predictable. Our future lives were truly unforeseeable. In a study reported by Kathleen Gerson in *Hard Choices,* women's predictions about how their working lives would turn out after having children were wrong two-thirds of the time, regardless of whether the woman predicted an expectation of domesticity or career. At your children's birth, who you are and what you want change irrevocably and unpredictably. What role you want to play—or rather, *roles*, since our current economy requires mothers to work more often than not—is not predetermined. You must forge your own role, values, and identity. In today's mothering world, you must not only *make it up,* but also then negotiate the desired job description with your friends, family, husband, and boss.

According to Anna Fels in *Necessary Dreams—Ambition in Women's Changing Lives,* it is the wife's ambition that is the first casualty of marriage, with or without children. She may still pursue ambitions, but in the vast majority of marriages, her ambition is secondary to the husband's. This is true even in cases when a wife earns more than the husband (which is now the case in a whopping 25 percent of marriages). The higher-earning wife is unlikely to attribute her success to ambition but instead chalks it up to luck or circumstances so as not to threaten, or fail to recognize and encourage, her husband's ambition. Fels' book scientifically substantiates that women are loathe to compete with men for rewards and recognition for two reasons: in many cases, she doesn't value self-promotion and isn't willing to self-promote as her male counterparts do; and she is afraid of the institutionalized backlash for women who steal the spotlight or an opportunity from a man. Consequently, men are more acknowledged and rewarded in the marketplace and, marriages depend more heavily on the man's success if only for practical reasons. As Fels states, "Marriage is a complicated bargain."

With a divorce rate of 50 percent maternal dependency may prove an unsafe assumption. Her career success becomes unexpectedly crucial. The best time for a woman to build her career may not come directly after an infant's birth. Unlike millions of years ago, children get more expensive as they grow older because they need much more than just food in order to thrive. And mothering is a bigger job because there is more information and complex training to pass on to offspring, as well as more status and protection to pursue on behalf of those offspring, all the way through young adulthood. In modern society, motherhood is the biggest lifetime predictor of poverty, which tells us that having a husband may not be a sufficient life plan.

Personal ambition seemed to be on a collision course
with my baby's needs. I wanted to care for my baby.
Damned if I don't, trapped if I do.
—SARAH BLAFFER HRDY

Maternal instinct establishes that a mother is by nature ambitious, *particularly after* the infancy phase of her children. Ambitions are nature's way of clueing you in to the fact that you're made up of your own talents, your unique vision, your voice, and your gift. Mother Nature gives you your calling to help you birth your personal contribution to the species, to the next generation. This " push" from nature is just as important as that first push so many years ago that brought your children into the world. Remember how strong your sex drive was when you were young? Consider this your "what's next?" drive. Now nature is pushing you to give the world your brainchild. And these days we often have upwards of 40 post-childbearing years to answer that call. It is an innate part of your maternal instinct to be ambitious and improve the quality of life for yourself and your children, so embrace your natural calling.

What's in You?

As a young woman, you came up against limitations and accepted them. You tackled big challenges and prevailed in college, in the workplace, and in establishing your own home and finding and marrying your husband. So you knew what you had in you. Or did you?

Perhaps you thought you couldn't cook or you were done with camping or hiking forever or it was too late to try your dream career. Even as you may have scaled back your career ambitions, the growing baby inside you helped you see that lots of things were possible.

The first time through your pregnancy was based on a natural mission, one beyond your life's comprehension. Your body was naturally ready, even though you may have felt personally unprepared. You were only dimly aware of what was in you, of the infrastructure that was in place: the hormones, the lactation ducts, the womb that sheltered your baby and the umbilicus that fed it as it grew. Your body was even prepared to handle the exponential growth. Who knew? Older women, midwives, and doctors told you these things were true, but you had no proof of it from your own experience. (Your bodily mission had been primarily romantic up until that time. Same body, new mission.) But because the childbirth mission is integral, authentic, and true everything fell into place more easily than you could imagine and you *were* ready to fulfill the mission naturally.

So there you were, big as a house, pushing the envelope, pressing yourself into service for a dual mission involving both your life and the baby's life. To call this phase in our lives "natural" was pressing the point. To Mother Nature, these things happen every day. In our experience, we fulfilled a grander mission than we knew we were capable of. What we had in us was far greater than we knew. It was perhaps natural but was at the same time exhilarating, bewildering, unpredictable, scary, and exciting. It begs the question: what is natural for a woman? For a mother? How far can her life naturally take her? Ambition is natural, but what about when the mission exceeds motherhood? You gave birth—you did that, so think what else you can do.

Anyone willing to rethink her limitations? Who's up for trying gourmet cooking, business management, or rocket science right now? Whatever limitations you have unconsciously or even consciously accepted, now is a good time to rethink them. No one can do everything her little heart desires in one lifetime, but apparently we have more in us than we knew and we can all do more than we ever thought—a whole lot more.

LABOR #29: BABY RESUME

Having a baby gave us life skills and work skills, like self-knowledge, management experience, and accountability. It helped give us authority and leadership skills and it helped us recruit support staff and identify growth areas. Fill out the job application below using only your pregnancy, birth, and mothering experience to convince the manager you're right for the job.

What is your job objective? (mission)

_____

_____

What is your relevant experience in:

- Day-to-day management of a project?

_____

_____

- Scheduling and coordination?

_____

_____

- Communication and team briefing?

_____

_____

- Strategy development?

_____

_____

- Resource allotment?

_____

_____

- Negotiating among departments?

_____

_____

- Budget projection and analysis?

_____

_____

- Financial planning?

_____

_____

- Organizational skills?

_____

_____

- Presenting and promoting team results?

_____

_____

- Developing opportunities?

_____

_____

- Team motivation?

_____

_____

- Vendor/contractor selection?

_____

_____

- Quality standards?

_____

_____

- Unsupervised project management?

_____

_____

Years in your current job?_____

Reason for leaving?_____

Can we contact your supervisor (yourself) for a good recommendation? _____

Would those who report to you (kids/husband/babysitter) recommend you? _____

Describe one incident that you feel portrays a unique strength that we should be aware of when considering you for this job.

_____

_____

What's Next?

It is perfectly natural to want big things, to desire a big life and big adventures. It is part of your mission to define which ambitions will bring you happiness, but if you have a long-held ambition that you've considered beyond your grasp it is *unnatural* to deny yourself the right to go for it. It is as unnatural as tamping down the overwhelming desire to push when nature calls on the delivery table.

Maybe your ambition is too lofty for your current life circumstances, but it's only too late if you don't start now. Consider this: Were you absolutely certain that when you began to labor and give birth that you could do it? Were you 100 percent sure it would go smoothly? Were you sure you could do this even though in the end you had only yourself to rely on? Didn't every mother understand at least on some level that she could die trying to give birth?

Of course, you had brought in experts and made sure you had a safe setting, precautionary equipment, and backup in case you needed a C-section. But it was still all up to you. You had to make it happen, take the risks, make the decisions, and make the baby.

Now how did you manage to get to that place where you felt safe to try the preposterous, dangerous, and *unnatural* feat of giving birth? By the time you were in labor you had personal and professional support. You had a coach and a team and you were ready.

At the time of birth, very few American mothers are alone. Once in a while, though, birth comes at an inopportune time and babies are born, quite naturally, on planes, in taxis, on cruise liners, etc. And people rush to help—perfect strangers help in the most intimate and dramatic of undertakings! So it is only natural that now, when you are undergoing a different sort of labor and are working hard to bring forth a very different "baby," people will step forward to help. Get out there. Tell people what you're trying to do and they will respond to your passion. As you bring your brainchild, your "baby" into being, people will be there for you. Strangers will help you do the impossible.

You've harbored your dream for a long time; maybe you even forgot for awhile and then let it resurface. There are ways to feed, shelter and grow that dream; there is a world of infrastructure to support most human dreams, like your body's hidden infrastructure or like the hospital, doctors, nurses and prenatal team. They may be waiting, untapped, but they are there for you. Naturally.

It's time to let your creations see the light of day.

How often do we hold back our one most precious, cherished desire? The very dream we have that could fulfill our mission is the same one that we're most afraid to share with anyone. Let your creation out—tell a friend, write it down, run it up a flagpole. You'll be amazed at who will respond, at how your dream will come to find its own supportive niche.

I knew it would take some pushing to make myself write this book. To find the support I needed, I offered a weekly seminar to my friends and neighbors. All of a sudden, I had 10 "midwives" and weekly deadlines to meet. Suddenly, I was growing my new life at the rate of one chapter per week.

In the end, if you need the help and intervention of Caesar (as in C-section) or you must dramatically call on a disinterested passerby to help you, the very fact that you are out there asking will miraculously attract support. Keep pushing and your infrastructure will naturally appear. Your limitations will dissolve and your new life *will* be born.

LABOR #30: DON'T LABOR ALONE

Who's on your team for the next phase of your life? How can you recruit others? Can you pay them or barter for their services? Who will be there to help, keep you on track, and keep you safe? Identify who you think you might need and then call friends or research one or more people to fill the necessary roles.

Lawyer

Accountant

Graphic designer

Copywriter

Babysitter

Life coach

Trainer
_____

Organizer
_____

Partner
_____

Bookkeeper
_____

Agent
_____

Household help
_____

Administrative intern
_____

Recognition

So that when I ask you to earn money and have a room of
your own, I am asking you to live in the presence of reality,
an invigorating life, it would appear.
—VIRGINIA WOOLF

In order to get to the next level of growth, we need to feel good about our-selves and our work. We need recognition to believe in ourselves and evolve—like a PokéMOM—to the next level. Fels identifies two fuels necessary to stoke ambition: mastery and recognition. According to Fels, women tend to frame their goals—even job goals—in terms of striving for their personal best or seek-ing self-fulfillment. We want to believe—and to have others around us believe—that money and recognition are not important. Fels argues that the desire to renounce recognition is acculturated in women, and yet without it ambition flags. If men get paid more for the same work and they get the pro-motions and the awards for our work, why bother? We rightfully feel resentful, demoralized, unmotivated, and self-doubting. *We* also need recognition to pros-per. We are accustomed to feeling invisible around the house. Think about it: when was the last time we truly took up space? When we were pregnant!

During pregnancy, we were proud because we knew we deserved others' respect. We gained weight and self-acceptance as well. As our bellies grew and our ankles swelled, we dressed more comfortably, didn't stand on ceremony, and didn't wait for approval. We felt valued and important as we accepted our foibles and our *bodies*. We lived comfortably with our limitations and once the birth was behind us and we moved into our children's newborn and infant stages, we felt competent, valued, capable, and needed. We attained a quiet, unquestioned authority as a *mother*. We achieved a self-love that was and is a wellspring for our thirsty souls. How do we dip our gourds and refresh our self-love now when we need it again? We do it through recognition.

Some big corporations bemoan the female brain drain and take steps to secure mothers' return to the workforce after a childbirth hiatus. Still, women find the offers unappealing because the corporate workplace is insufficiently flexible for anyone—man or woman—to raise a family, run a home and feel that it was all worthwhile. Meanwhile, men are doing less and still getting more praise for what they do at home (Fels says that if a man does 36 percent of the household work, he feels like he's done 50 percent and gets hailed as a hero). At work, men are categorically more recognized—facially, verbally, financially—and given better, more interesting tasks to perform. Without sufficient recognition, women drop out or don't even try.

And since so many of us have college and advanced degrees, career experience, and ambitions, we feel it is our own failing—lack of motivation, a character flaw, or laziness—that keeps us from succeeding in the workplace.

How can we get the missing recognition that fuels our ambition and makes work emotionally and financially satisfying? It is not unfeminine to want success. It is *human* to crave the recognition and attention that fuels ambition and success.

OUTSIDE RECOGNITION

Look to the masters and don't discredit their methods. Men get recognition by asking for it. Toot your own horn, be visible, and network with important people. Why we disdain what obviously works I don't know. I myself have felt that glad-handing was a waste of my time and not as important as the actual work. I've even characterized networking as a superficial, tawdry attempt at self-promotion. But where was my time better spent? In working late without compensation? Why didn't I employ my famous relational ability to tend my invisible network?

If you're not interested in corporate culture, consider counterculture. Start your own business. Because it is nearly impossible for a woman to get the recognition she needs in the workplace (not to mention the flexibility) many women have opted out. (Consider renting *Baby Boom* starring Diane Keaton. Better yet, look at Diane Keaton's own track record. When roles for women were scarce, she directed ten movies and produced nine. See www.imdb.com)

Women-owned businesses are flourishing, representing one in four new businesses opened every year. If you have skills or an idea or would like to consider a franchise, opt out of the corporate culture and lead your own.

SELF-RECOGNITION

Sometimes we have to make a good living and we have to recognize the obvious: we're not being credited for the good job we're doing. How do we get satisfaction? How do we face continuing in the job with limited recognition and no immediate change on the horizon?

Consider all the great sources of recognition that women are masters of, such as journaling, prayer, time alone to process, a supportive group of women, an Unpregnancy group, a mentor, a life coach or online at www.unpregnancy.com. All of these methods can give you back the recognition and support you need and the insight you need to envision an ambitious path up or out of your current situation.

As mothers it is our fortune to have life experience to draw on. Pregnancy and birth facilitated self-love. We were able to remove ourselves from our usual standards of judgment and scorn. Instead of criticizing ourselves, we marveled at our abilities and discoveries as our pregnancies progressed. We adopted a kinder internal voice. We accepted that this was a journey we'd never been on before, so we didn't expect a certain standard of behavior or achievement. This is not to say we didn't push ourselves. Many of us lived our public lives very much as if we weren't pregnant, especially the first time. Doing just as much as we had always done and doing it as well as we always had made us pretty proud of ourselves. The simple fact of being pregnant and doing just what we were doing, achieving in a day simply what we could achieve in a day, activated our internal cheering sections.

How are these next nine months different from those months? How is your Unpregnancy different from your pregnancy? Where is your internal cheering section now? Have you ever been Unpregnant before? Have you ever lived these nine months before? Can you allow yourself to be kinder and more encouraging? Can you gift yourself with your mothering voice rather than your self-critical voice? (*Your mother's voice?*) Most of us consider ourselves good mothers who have certainly done the best we knew how for our children. Give yourself that same gift: allow yourself to be deserving of your own brand of mother-love and recognition.

LABOR #31: STAR IN YOUR OWN LIFE

Be the star of your own life. Take up space, self-promote, get recognized. Prepare for a confident self-presentation. This is the interview, this is the late night when the work gets done and the credit is being handed out. How will you square your shoulders, shake someone's hand, allow yourself to be complimented, and take credit? How will your star rise?

Many of us are so sure that we are not worthy—for various private reasons—that we refuse to allow pictures of ourselves to be taken. We flee when the cameras come out and quail when we see ourselves in a photo. Women I know consider it not only reasonable but laudable to be modest and demure in this manner. Do you really think you want to be *absent* from the documentation of your life? Don't you think when your kids look back at their childhood pictures they'll want to see you there? Are we so hateful of our bodies that we can't inhabit our own family photos? It's time to reacquaint yourself with your physical image and give yourself a hug.

PHOTO TIME

If you feel you never look good in a picture, collect a variety of photos of yourself, some you like, some you hate, and some that are so-so. Create an exhibit of the photos and allow yourself time to get to know that face and that body. This is the face and body that people who love you *love*. Why not find a way to love your whole self? Perhaps you feel as though you've just never been photographed well; you might then treat yourself to a professional photography session. Ask the photographer to look at your amateur snapshots and comment on why you might look the way you do in the photos. Ask the photographer shoot several rolls of film of just you, black and white and color, in many poses and with a variety of facial expressions. Exhibit these pictures privately or publicly someplace where you can spend time looking at them and accepting them as yourself—your beautiful, loved self.

MIRROR TIME

Wearing business clothes, spend some time in front of the mirror. Stop and greet yourself, sit, stand, and shake hands. Begin talking and watch yourself. Be kind. Allow yourself to lovingly take in your image and speak to yourself kindly. Look at yourself in the mirror and repeat two or three statements that are honest yet kind. Be specific. "I look good" is not as good as "I look reliable" "This look makes me look interesting and creative."

REALITY SHOW

Spend some time observing real women who work in your intended profession. Look at their real bodies in real outfits. They're not digitally altered and they don't have a team of professionals dressing and primping them each moment. (If you feel ashamed about your body size, remember that most people don't care if you're fat, they only care if they're fat.)

Then take some time to dress your real body—get rid of things that don't fit, that you wish would fit or that you're keeping in case they fit some time in the future. Buy clothes that are appropriate for you. You might even seek out the assistance of a professional shopper at a major department store.

Forget before-and-after pictures—the "During" is what counts. Taking it one day at a time, keep a photo journal of the changes in yourself as you approach your goal. While you may not feel proud of some of the pictures, being able to visually chart your progress will help you feel proud of your physical image, over time.

Extreme Makeover

When was your last extreme makeover? I'll venture to guess that it was during your last pregnancy. A crack team of professionals—dressers (maternity shops), hairstylists, doctors and counselors, coaches and nurses—all prepared you for the dramatic reveal: the new you. Every change was played out in the public eye like some reality show. And in the end, you were slouching on a couch in your husband's big shirt and stretchy pants, with your waistline out to here. Yet you were satisfied with the results.

Now your makeover is moving in the opposite direction by making you presentable, impressive, and employable, hopefully without any loss of satisfaction.

We're talking more than just your wardrobe and presentation, though; your life needs an extreme makeover. You've slogged through six months of personal goal attainment and three more of family tweaking. Are you satisfied with the results? Is your whole family ready to push you out into the world and clap wildly at the reveal of the new you?

A mother cannot do it all alone.

Yet how can you enjoy work success if you're punished at home? And how can you continue in unrewarding or difficult work if you don't get the recognition you need from friends and family? Your quality of life may suffer for the sake of finances, or maybe the opposite is true. Maybe you work because you need the money; maybe you need the recognition to help make home life more bearable. Both are valid, ambitious reasons to seek work outside your home.

Assuming you're pursuing an ambition and looking for recognition and reward, make sure you've managed the process and expectations reasonably before you begin your life makeover.

LABOR #32: TGIM?

After the baby came, many of us left the workplace, but some of us soldiered on, resenting its intrusion into our cherished motherhood. Still others loved work and concealed a case of TGIM—Thank God It's Monday. (I remember thinking: *At least at work, I can go to the bathroom when I have to and have a cup of coffee when I want to.*) Regardless of your immediate past in the work world, you're now contemplating a change. You're going to put yourself out there and try to achieve something that's really meaningful to you. It will be hard and possibly unpleasant at times. Why do it? Why not? Make your list below.

TGIM (JOB PROS)   **TGIF (JOB CONS)**

_____   _____

_____   _____

_____   _____

_____   _____

_____   _____

_____   _____

_____   _____

_____   _____

Look carefully at your lists. Can you mitigate the TGIF aspects of your intended role? Can you amplify the TGIM feeling, the joy of the job? If not now, when? Sometimes there's an uphill climb to get what you want, but the view from the top is worthwhile. Look for a tangible reward or change within a time frame (the end of your third trimester?) so you can alleviate the pressure and deliver yourself a joyful outcome.

Go to the Head of the Class

Mother Nature is both an easygoing and a harsh taskmaster. She provides and takes away. When you consider what is in your nature, take into account your experiences of being pregnant, giving birth, and nursing your newborn. Allow yourself to embrace all of your years, all of your accomplishments.

Consider your unmet needs and realize that you're deserving of having those needs met. You are lovable, right down to the stray hairs on your chin and the breasts that sag from pregnancy and nursing.

Nature is no perfectionist, but she is ambitious and productive. As we strive to love and grow, we'll come to know that we are proud and able. Pregnancy gave us that gift and motherhood presses us to fulfill our potential, hear our ambitions and answer our callings. Answer the "what's next?" drive!

A little-noticed and oft-overlooked fact of nature: Mammals—large and small, male and female, from mouse to tiger, from camel and lioness to apes and humans—are all named for the mammary gland and our unique ability to nourish our young. Mammalia, the entire class of warm-blooded, thinking, feeling animals, is named for our breasts and milk ducts. What makes us the primary class of animals is our maternal instinct—we invest in each child, nurse and nurture and teach and help our children better their quality of life. We are mammals and we go to the head of the class.

Keep Your Eyes on the Prize

Pregnancy demands a successful outcome. As Elizabeth Cady Stanton said about winning women the right to vote, "Failure is not possible." During pregnancy your dedication is comprehensive. You go to extreme lengths to narrow the odds of any failure. Your whole being leans into this job—mitigating risk, finding support for your new needs, nurturing the pregnancy and finding out everything you need to know to have a safe, comfortable and *productive* pregnancy. You prepare and you invest in yourself. This pregnancy lesson is easily overlooked because despite your devoted apprenticeship in pregnancy you were so enthralled with every blip of data, each pearl of wisdom, any candid story of a symptom conquered or fear allayed that you hardly noticed how much time and energy you invested. You were in it to win.

How many pregnancy books did you read? How many doctors' appointments did you have? What about childbirth classes? How about the countless other "experts" you consulted and logged hundreds of hours with—your friends, female relatives, and strangers on the bus?

Pregnancy is the poster child for motivation!

From the day the stick turned blue, you were charged with finding out everything you needed to know and you talked to anyone who could help, including perfect strangers. Shy and retiring no more, you let your need to know overwhelm your timidity or distaste for networking. There you were— asking for help, favors, and information, researching on the internet, hinting at embarrassing fears about your body, yourself, your worthiness to mother a child. What if right now you knew you wanted to be a children's book illustrator; wouldn't you feel timid about asking a known illustrator in your town for help or advice? Would you feel like you had the natural right to inquire?

More than talking, you listened when you were pregnant. You opened your mind to new ideas, new expectations; you tried new things and quit bad habits. You entertained new ways of thinking about yourself, considering your abilities, and praising your achievements. Commitment built momentum, which built your self-esteem, which fueled your successes.

Soon you were *showing.* Maybe only you could see it at first, but it was only a matter of time before others noticed your little belly promising *big* changes.

The pregnancy began to feel more real. You persevered and were consistent. You came to understand how to stick with something for a long period of time, allowing yourself a moderate and forgiving approach. You stuck with your new rules for yourself—the rules of pregnancy—but gave yourself divine permission to allow other rules and expectations to slide. Some of us happily quit exercising. Some of us felt daily chocolate was a mental health ritual. Some of us took a daily nap, got our nails done regularly, and scheduled a weekly massage or facial. One good friend of mine remarked on how lush life is when you don't have to worry about your two biggest fears: gaining weight or getting pregnant. No guilt, no recrimination, no scolding, no worries.

Not so fast . . . no worries? We had plenty of worries, just not the usual ones. Our negativity emerged out of our vulnerability about things like birth defects, delivery problems, preeclampsia, gestational diabetes, and whether or not we could *do* it. We had a lot to tackle—real and imagined.

It's no wonder you became an amateur sleuth to rival Nancy Drew. You needed clues and information about how to transform your life from the happy-go-lucky girl to a mom (and all that that implied).

When self-help information didn't fill in the whole picture, you willingly paid for training, guidance, classes, and professional help like doctors' appointments, birth classes, pregnancy fitness classes, and special self-care indulgences. Did you have a budget for these items?

And whether you've already put your kids through college or just written the check for a Gymboree Mommy and Me class, it's already begun. Many of us have paid handsomely for tap lessons, SAT prep courses, and Tae Kwon Do, not to mention braces, doctors, and sports equipment and coaches for the kids, yet we flinch when it comes to spending on ourselves. (They get all the money.) We tell ourselves, *We're building toward their future.* What future are you building for yourself? This is your life we're talking about.

Pregnancy committed all of your resources—ingenuity, time and money to ensure a good outcome. A similar level of commitment—to networking, to spending real time *and* money—will deliver an excellent Unpregnancy outcome, too. Consider your new rules of Unpregnancy: do something toward your goal each day; moderate your internal voice to be loving; baby yourself;

celebrate the successes; reach out for help; rethink your expectations; honor your mission; and let some of your old rules and chores go. Consider it part of your job as a good mom and a shining example to your kids of any age, to build a happy, productive future for yourself and give yourself the time and permission to devote to exploring it now.

Anything else can wait. You'll still be around to make magnificent meals after your Unpregnancy (and you might be more in the mood to do so) so increase your takeout budget, if that's what it takes to give you the flexibility you need now.

Open yourself to new ideas, longer conversations, more laughing, sharing, seeking, and researching with friends, strangers, friends of friends, relatives, and professionals.

Consider what professionals could help you reach your goals. In my first Unpregnancy, I had three goals. My first was to lose weight, my second was to restore the fun in my marriage, and the third was to consider whether I could afford to risk income and find a safe way to switch careers. In my first trimester, my level of dedication alone was sufficient to get me on track for dieting and exercise. I was in the zone and I lost steadily. My success fueled momentum and more steady success. I got so ambitious that I wanted to spread the spirit to my children's diets. Our family physician recommended a new nutritionist for one of my daughters. Alarms went off in my head. Because of some bad diet experiences in my childhood, I insisted on seeing this new nutritionist myself: I didn't want my happy, centered, if a little overweight daughter subjected to any bad programming. Because of a protective instinct on my daughter's behalf, I looked into our insurance coverage for nutritionists and realized that we were covered. Why hadn't I looked into that years earlier and availed myself of help long before? Visiting a nutritionist was a very positive experience for both of us, but I would have continued to deprive myself of that tool out of ignorance had it not been for my daughter's need. We need to step up and help *ourselves*. I wised up for my second and third trimester goals and I sought out seminars to help me open my mind to new approaches to old problems. Unpregnancy is an approach to your transformation and you will likely need tools and input based on your individual goals.

With this Unpregnancy, consider yourself *pregnant* with your unborn dream. If you don't learn now how to give it life, it could be stillborn. Your Unpregnant gift to yourself and to the world could die and with it an exciting part of you and who you wish to become.

LABOR #33: YOU'RE WORTH IT

Let's add up the investment of time and money you made during a single pregnancy.

TIME

How many pregnancy books did you read? _____ x 3 hours per book = _____ hours

How much time did you spend on pregnancy websites or reading emailed pregnancy newsletters or brochures and magazine articles? _____ x 40 weeks = _____ hours

Did you keep a pregnancy journal (online or in a notebook)? How much time per week? _____ x 40 weeks = _____ hours

How many doctors' appointments did you have? _____ x 1- 2 hours each = _____ hours

What about Lamaze or childbirth classes? How many? _____ x 2 hours each = _____ hours

Visit the hospital in advance of birth = _____ hours

Meet the backup physician = _____ hours

What other precautions did you take or what other time investments?

- ○ Daily care rituals
- ○ Stay in bed for portion of the pregnancy
- ○ Daily obligations—e.g., vitamins, lotions
- ○ Quit working early
- ○ Eat healthily
- ○ Pregnancy fitness routine
- ○ Quit exercising
- ○ Quit/cut down drinking
- ○ Quit/cut down smoking
- ○ Other

Estimate your total time investment from the above list and other time expenditures: _____ hours

TOTAL _____ hours

Divide total by 40 weeks: _____ /40 weeks = _____ average time per week

Consider this weekly investment of time toward your pregnancy. Is your Unpregnancy investment similar?

MONEY

Estimate the cost of your pregnancy books: _____ books x $15.00 each = $ _____

What were your medical costs? (not covered by health insurance)
Deductibles, co-pays, electives, like paying for TV, single room in the
hospital, assurances, like extra sonograms, not covered by
health insurance: $ _____

How much do you recall paying for childbirth classes? $ _____

Did you pay for smoking cessation or other self-help programs? $ _____

Maternity clothes estimate: $ _____

Maternity products—like stretch mark creams, prenatal vitamins, etc.: $ _____

Exercise programs: $ _____

Costs for other indulgences, like massages, taxis, takeout:

Baby monitors/music in utero, etc.: $ _____

Other professional costs: doula, midwife, counselor: $ _____

Total Cost: $ _____

Cost per week: $ _____ /40 = $ _____

Once you've added up the amount of money spent during your pregnancy figure that dollar for dollar, you deserve to spend that same amount on your Unpregnancy. If your pregnancy expenditures seem very high, consider how much of that amount you could realistically earmark for your Unpregnancy goals. Or take another approach—project what expenses you might incur as an investment in yourself and your goals and use them to create a budget.

What steps could you take to further your Unpregnancy goals? Considering the investment you made in maternity—not to mention the ongoing investments we all make in our children's education, entertainment and futures—what can you afford to invest in yourself during this Unpregnancy to ensure success, mitigate risk and prepare for the impending changes in your life?

- **Seek a professional's help and advice**
  - Career counselor
  - Life coach
  - Take a class on the subject
  - Consider a degree in your subject
- **Research costs**
  - Lunch budget—informational lunches with networked contacts
  - Seminars
  - Subscriptions to trade/topical magazines
  - Books, magazines, other research
- **Travel and lodging**
  - Trade shows, for research and networking
  - Site evaluation
  - Hiatus: fellowships/semesters away from the family
- **Investing in the new you costs**
  - Tools of the trade
  - Clothes for the new you
  - Production costs—printing, painting, binding, placement, exhibit launching, advertising, marketing, and publicity

Now work out a budget below. Take the necessary steps in your family to approve the budget; whether that entails really thinking it through and coming to a firm approval by yourself or sharing the numbers and the rationale behind them with a partner, get the amount approved.

Your Unpregnancy Budget $ _____ (Approved)

It's Not a Contest

During pregnancy we exhibited unfailing dedication. According to the March of Dimes, 27 out of 28 births are healthy deliveries without birth defects, and the causes of 60 percent to 70 percent of birth defects are unknown. Understandably we approach pregnancy with serious dedication and spare no effort or expense to bring a safe, healthy life into this world. We do everything we can to ensure our best efforts toward success and yet we can only do so much. Not everything is under our control.

Fear of the unknown can be scary during pregnancy and social pressure and values hold us to carefully prescribed pregnancy behavior. Here's the pregnancy surprise: despite avidity, we are moderate and positive and because others know that we're on a requisite course of self-sacrifice during the nine long months of pregnancy, they support us with positivity. Think about the last time you announced you were going to eat healthier. And when, two days later, you decided to sneak some ice cream—or cookies or cake or potato chips or French fries—how did you and your family react? *Are you sure you should be having that? You're going to regret that. You're the one who said . . . .*palpable negativity.

That's when my inner toddler perks up and I get very defiant. *You shut up. You're not the boss of me.* But the resentment and anger I feel resonates in my subconscious and next thing you know a reasonable indulgence becomes a regrettable overindulgence. Some brownie mix licked from my finger during baking becomes a double helping of brownies downed guiltily later (without much pleasure, I might add).

What you and everyone around you seemed to know instinctively during your pregnancy is this: moderation and positivity are key for long-term success. If you are going to learn to ice skate, you have to expect to fall. Scolding yourself never helps.

In pregnancy, you're not training for a marathon or preparing for the Iditarod across the frozen Alaskan tundra. Dedication? Sure. Commitment? Absolutely. Go to great lengths? Nothing is too much for my healthy baby. But keep in mind that in order to go the distance, moderation is key. Pace yourself. Be realistic. A little slipup is not a catastrophe. *I'm doing great—and that chocolate cake was magnificent, didn't you think so, baby?* You actually feel *good* about the small indulgences. You don't scold yourself or alert your subconscious to sabotage your efforts, so the indulgences stay *small*. The gift from pregnancy that you'll need in your Unpregnancy is to recall and reapply the high level of dedication tempered with moderation and forgiveness. We tend to have rules for ourselves—about eating, about promptness, about exercise regimens, about performance expectations at work and home, and about how much we should do in a day. And if we break one of these rules, if we lapse, we can't forgive ourselves. Our critical voice kicks in and we begin a stressful internal argument. We can be very hard on ourselves.

Look at your efforts in Unpregnancy and moderate your negative reaction to a slipup. Try to catch your inner critic and change its message. During pregnancy you were able to do this naturally. Try a new response to internal reproach: congratulate yourself for being loving toward yourself. Consider yourself as blameless as a baby, as faultless as a pregnant mother. For a moment, try talking to yourself as you remember addressing your unborn baby—*hey baby, are you okay in there?* Do you hear your tone of voice? Don't you deserve that kind, gentle voice? Maybe you could give your unborn self or goal self a sweet name. *Hey writer!* or *Whoa, Slim, you're gonna like that cookie* or *My inner-techie will conquer this problem.*

Forgiveness also has to be extended to things that are out of your control. We acknowledge in pregnancy how much we can't control but somehow don't accept similar realities in our grown-up life and pursuits. We want total control and we want it now. We want a quick fix or a pill to make it happen. Even though we know this can't be true—or everyone would be a slim millionaire with a fulfilling sex life—we don't internalize how long it will take and how hard it will be to achieve our goals.

We get revved up on willpower and excitement but then it fizzles out before the nine months (maybe nine weeks? nine days?) are up. It's like baby fat—if it took nine months to gain, it will take at least nine months to lose. Moderate your expectations, forgive your lapses, and stay the course.

Don't be discouraged if you have long times with no apparent progress. Sometimes progress isn't visible. (Consider your darling, developing baby. Miracles of growth and progress were happening just below the surface, but did you focus on your stretch marks instead?)

Make sure your progress indicators *are* under your control. For example, you can't control or predict weight loss. (We do the math in our head so fast—*By Christmas I'll be x and by Spring I'll be ready for that bikini.* We tell ourselves, *If Doctor So-and-So says I can, then I can.* We deny our own experience in order to feel in control of what is uncontrollable. No wonder we crash so hard when it fails.)

Your performance indicators should be small steps that have proven to add up to your desired goal. Sticking with the weight loss example, your indicators could be the following:

* **Taking your multivitamin every day**
* **Serving yourself meals that are fruit or vegetable on half of the plate**
* **Keeping a weight chart**
* **Exercising three to five times a week, for at least 30 minutes**
* **Having three servings of calcium and/or a calcium supplement daily**
* **Keeping your appointments with a nutritionist**
* **Graciously accepting a compliment as proof of progress**

Don't allow your entire effort to hinge on one number—like a weigh-in—that is out of your control. Give yourself internal and external praise for maintaining small steps. Forgive yourself a small misstep and keep walking—because small steps add up.

When it comes to indulgence, I caution you to avoid indulging in comparisons. Do not compare yourself to what the book says you should have or could have been able to achieve. Don't compare yourself to your mother, your friend or your sister. Don't allow someone else to compare your effort—or pain or experience or success—to her own either. It belittles both your efforts and experiences. No one can compare pain, hunger, perseverance or circumstance. No one can decide what *you* should have done based on *her* experiences.

Imitate, try new things, and listen to other people's experiences as possibilities for experimentation or success. But trust your own experience, even if Doctor So-and-So says otherwise. No two labors are alike just as no two successful outcomes—or any two precious babies—are alike.

LABOR #34: ALTER EGO

Moderation, forgiveness, and praise for small steps help you to go the distance. How can we moderate our critical inner voices and keep encouragement flowing?

❋ **Remember to moderate your inner voice and self-messaging**

❋ **When you feel that sinking feeling of disappointment in yourself or hear a rebuke coming on, adopt your "hey baby" voice**

❋ **Name your (w)inner self**

- Slim
- Sexy Sue
- Boss Lady
- Willow (strong and supple)
- River (Goes with the flow, carves out territory)
- Oscar, Emmy or Grammy (for the prizes you hope to be nominated for one day)
- Nobel (ditto)
- Dr. <u>Your Name Here</u>
- Bess (for best at anything, bestseller, etc.)

❋ **Pick a Song**

- What song typifies your effort? *Climb Every Mountain*? *I Will Survive*? *I Am Woman*? *Celebrate*? Sheryl Crow's *A Change Would Do You Good*? The Beatles' *Long and Winding Road*?
- When you're happy and you know it, sing a song
- When you're scolding yourself, sing over the noise

Finding the Right Tools

You've entered the Unpregnancy zone. You're trying something that is new and, quite frankly, a little scary. There's so much to learn that you don't know where to start and you don't see how you can have the life you dream of. *Like I could just get on a plane to Hollywood and sell a movie script*. But your goals are lofty and important to you and vital to your future happiness.

Suppose you need to figure out something you've never even considered before in order to meet your goal. You don't have the foggiest notion where to start. Can you ever remember feeling like that during your pregnancy?

Can you remember feeling as if you were in over your head? Can you remember not having all the answers or not even having all the questions? Well, now you're Unpregnant. And if you're doing it right, you're in over your head. There's no turning back and time's a wastin'.

What tools are you going to need to get from here to there? How can you be certain you are making progress toward your goal if you're not sure what it's going to take?

You get started. You're determined to get there so you do a little bit of everything—panic, question, research, pray, take a class, ask a friend, ask your mom, ask your dog. If you hope to make forward progress, you keep track of what you've done, what you found out, the methods you could be doing, have done, might be able to do, and/or people you could call or talk to about how to get there.

These are the many tools for tracking a successful, productive Unpregnancy.

Blogging—visit www.unpregnancy.com and create a blog. (Just in case you've been experiencing child-induced brain fog, "blog" is short for Web logue, i.e., posting your journal pages on the web.) You can post your experiences on a daily or weekly basis and it will help you track your progress. If you have a digital camera or scanner, you can even post photos that show progress toward your goal. Documenting a journey can keep it on track, build in a support group for your efforts, and keep you in touch with progress, even when you may be temporarily despondent. Linking to other people's blogs will help connect you to other Unpregnant women who have undertaken your goals or something similar. Reading other women's experiences can help you gain insight, information, and inspiration.

Morning Journal—If you haven't already begun your Morning Journal, I highly recommend you do so *tomorrow morning*. Unlike blogging, this is a strictly private journaling adventure. It can be a finished piece on how you're feeling at any given stage of Unpregnancy, but it is more likely to be a place to vent each morning. There is nothing very charming or interesting about a

Morning Journal except to the person writing it. It is a place to record an unobstructed stream of consciousness; in precisely three pages a day you can rid yourself of the "morning sickness" of Unpregnancy, that unfocused anxiety, stress, pettiness or nagging dream from the night before. It's *I have to call the plumber* four days in a row or *I hate it when Max gets like this* or *What will I say to Beth's teacher?*

When I keep a Morning Journal I find my days are relieved of that free-floating negativity and a little more focused on what I want my day to be about. Since I've written down the mundane *call the plumber,* I'm more likely to do it that day and less likely to let it stress me out when it resurfaces as something I failed to do. Since I've delved into my feelings about *Max* and *Beth's teacher* I'm more likely to come to understand what's bugging me about our interactions and express it productively. My days are more focused on *my* priorities. In fact, my Morning Journal identifies my priorities for me. What is on my conscious list is not always my most important task for the day. As I let my petty concerns and small ideas pour onto the page, I empty myself of guilt or worry and my real priorities let themselves be known. (As obvious as a hungry, frantic baby, my true emotional needs cry out and find their way onto the page, demanding my attention.) Often I've only become aware of a sizable energy drain when it shows up day after day in my Morning Journal. If I didn't see it there, I couldn't have recognized how imperative it was becoming for me to address or change the situation for my own peace of mind.

Mother and Mentors—Older women are a great resource, one we tend to overlook. Their rules and values may be so different from yours that you may give up on these women before you're able to seek their wisdom and experience. What they have to offer you, you certainly also have to offer younger women. And so it goes. Overlook differences in wardrobe and daily routines and ask for real help in the form of ideas, contacts, advice, cheerleading, and advocacy. And then don't forget to pass along advice to younger women who are seeking to better their lives and options.

Friends—Many of us hate to impose on a friend unless it is in a pre-approved way. You can ask a friend to bake for a bake sale or pick up your kid after school when you're sick or running late. But what if your friend is a lawyer and you want legal advice? What if she's a publicist who reps celebrities? Can you ask her to give Faith Hill your demo? Where you draw the lines of imposition is your own affair. However, I will say that every woman I know could impose more; she would be welcome to ask for help and the person being asked the favor would be grateful to help. Is this because I only know superwomen? Yes, it's true. Like most women they routinely give more than they get and have brownie points built up skyhigh. They're so concerned about imposing that they can't ask and when they do get up the nerve to ask, they don't ask for the help they really want.

The only time an imposition is truly an imposition is when you don't have the equity in the relationship—i.e., the friend doesn't like you or appreciate you to the degree that the task assumes. This is why it is hard to ask for help. "What if" turns into the proof I hoped to avoid facing: she doesn't like me as much as I'd like to think.

To ameliorate that risk, when you ask a favor, prepare in advance—have a demo that is worthy of Faith Hill, cue up your legal questions. And be prepared for a polite no. It's not the end of the world or even the end of your friendship. There could be a perfectly good reason she can't say yes and there could also be other ways she could help you.

- **Use your friends first (that's what friends are for).**
- **Share your frustrations for feedback and ideas.**
- **Barter time with a friend to help further a goal.**
- **Ask for help in achieving your goals**
  - Once you've prepared enough to have a legitimate reason to ask
  - Once you're prepared for a no without emotional fallout
  - Once you've considered other, lesser ways your friend could help you
- **Ask for what you need simply and without apology.**

Tracking Tools—There are many ways to tell a story. You need to track your progress, your ups your downs, your hopes and fears. When I was losing weight, I decided to take a Polaroid snapshot of myself every few days, because the before and after photos did not do my efforts justice. So I decided that the best way to see the process very clearly would be to create a flip-book of my weight loss. Now if I ever want to see why I shouldn't put the weight back on

I just run the flip-book in reverse and I have graphic evidence of how long and hard the process would be to reverse the consequences.

❋ **What tracking methods could you employ to chart the small steps that are under your control for your Unpregnancy**

❋ **As appropriate for your goals, think about doing any of these:**

- Daily stars or points for progress indicators
- Progress charts
- Flow charts
- Time tables/agendas/critical path
- Morning Journal
- Photo journaling
- File/notebook/computer-based organizer software
- Money Jar—stash the cash you would have spent to buy cigarettes or some similar indulgence
- Other _____

Professional Help—So you're not a big movie producer, novelist, painter, photographer, restaurateur, talk show host, founder of a nonprofit organization, business owner, work-at-home entrepreneur, or trapeze artist—yet. So far you're just Unpregnant. You've been pursuing contentedness, downtime, a mission statement, and sense of your brand. You've been taking parts of your life back and giving with a strict giving policy so you'll have more to invest in other avenues of adventure. Where to begin? What are the tools? Who will teach you how to use them? Unlike my namesake in *Pretty Woman* you don't have a mentor teaching you which is the salad fork and how to dress so you can shop in the snooty Beverly Hills boutiques. You don't have a trained professional wielding the forceps, the boom mike, the spice mill, the close-up camera, the C5103 forms, the articles of incorporation, or the thingy... How will you figure out how to do those things?

LABOR #35: TOOLS OF THE TRADE

❋   Look into classes, seminars, and ongoing professional help to support your efforts.

❋   Talk to a life coach about how you might work together.

❋   Look over the many tracking methods identified in this chapter and commit to one or more methods for documenting your Unpregnancy.

   • Blogging

   • Morning Journal

   • Mothers and Mentors

   • Friends

   • Tracking Tools

   • Professional Help

❋   Commit to the small steps and create a chart or method to track and praise those small victories that will bring you closer to success.

❋   Create enough pages of your preferred chart to last for the entire 40 weeks of effort to clearly illustrate how long you will sustain your labor.

You're in the Club

You've survived the arduous hazing ritual of pregnancy and birth and now you're initiated. You're a mother. The secret handshake—like I need to tell *you*—is a hesitant step forward and then an abrupt halt while each mom unconsciously checks for yogurt or spit-up before extending her hand for a warm, friendly handshake.

Everyone loves a pregnant woman because she is so full of hope and potential. They know what you're in for (the good, the bad and the ugly outfits) and they're excited about your future. People you saw as grown-ups, bosses, *old* only a short while before (and who seemingly saw you as *so young*) now begin to treat you as a peer. There's an odd camaraderie among mothers of all ages and generations. The gap is bridged and a surprising bond begins to develop as you each allow the other to share wisdom, concerns, insights, and ideas and to enter each other's circle of influence.

New and surprising sources of support can develop quickly when you're pregnant. New respect, new bonds, and new friendships can blossom based on how colleagues, neighbors, and others respond and encourage you in your time of need.

Indeed, just as in pregnancy, groups can be a source of great help and inspiration during your Unpregnancy. Joining an Unpregnancy group online (www.unpregnancy.com) can help you adhere to the positive, self-fueling approach to goal achievement that we learned in pregnancy. It is important to keep that experience fresh as other methods push us toward self-deprivation and self-chastising. If you keep pregnancy as your guiding force in your Unpregnancy, you won't be able to scold yourself into compliance.

Depending on your own Unpregnancy goals, there may be a national group to support your endeavor or you may find a group to support your specific goal. As the members of groups like Alcoholics and Overeaters Anonymous or Smokenders or Weight Watchers know, most of life's biggest challenges have been faced down by millions before you and will pose a challenge to millions after you. If you can't find a group, create one or look for a support group online. Cancer survivors and family members, domestic violence victims, and Adult Children of Alcoholics all offer support online and in local chapters.

As an Unpregnant woman, incorporating any other group's approach to your goal is like a pregnant woman joining a nonpregnancy fitness class. You'll need to be cautious. Your Unpregnancy relies on maintaining a positive approach, a kinder internal voice and a moderate, realistic, paced approach. Don't do anything that could hurt you or your Unpregnant mindset. If you have questions about whether a group is going to be a positive and supportive experience for you in your Unpregnancy, visit www.motherhoodtootherhood.com and post a question. There's got to be another mom out there who has been through that goal set and can share her experience (in gory detail). You're in the club.

In the second trimester, you're facing down different demons, ones not necessarily your own who seem to take shape between you and your loved ones. Disagreements, petty comments, defiance, or a show of will can all be damaging, frustrating, and draining. To consider how to approach your hopes for your friends and family, groups can help you too. You might try therapy sessions, marriage retreats, church, or scouting weekends with the kids. You might even try a cross-country tour or a prearranged bike trip through your area or the area you grew up in. In this stage, remember to be generous with your loved ones.

In the third trimester, you're bedeviled by a new set of problems that groups can help you resolve. Most professional or community groups have a unique lingo, unspoken expectations, and a dress code which can seem foreign and formidable as you try to fit in and learn the ropes. You've got to learn the exotic vocabulary, nicknames, anagrams, and acronyms.

There was certainly a time when you didn't know what swaddling was or why preeclampsia would clamp you in bed. And when it comes to contraptions, we all expressed milk and sterilized bottles or managed nursing bras on little or no sleep. You need to find the right tools for your journey—and you gotta know the territory.

How do you begin to walk the walk and talk to the talk? Professional associations—national or local—can help give you the code words to gain entry to the clubhouse. Many include magazine subscriptions that will keep you up to date on the people you should know about and the deals that are being made, who's got fresh new ideas, who's coming and who's going. Associations often host working lunches and networking parties that will give you opportunities to adapt your self-presentation and allow you to try out your new identity and your Unpregnant self (bring *Bess* out for everyone to see).

Start an Unpregnancy Group—Another essential support for the Unpregnant woman is the equivalent of that one friend who is also having a baby—your Unpregnant friend. Think about doing your Unpregnancy with a friend or joining forces with women who are following the rules of Unpregnancy. Meet for coffee or lunch to discuss your progress, fears and experiences. Form an informal exercise group to make sure you hit the road three times a week.

Get together with a group of friends regularly throughout your Unpregnancy. If you can't find the women to create a dedicated group, join a women's club in your area to meet with them and talk about what you're striving to do. Or go to your library and ask for their help in promoting a group based on the book *Motherhood to Otherhood* and Unpregnancy. Like-minded women will give you perspective, pressure, and the support you need to make big things happen. Go to www.motherhoodtootherhood.com to find an online community of Unpregnant women who can supplement the real thing.

Fantasize/Visualize

Shopping for little baby booties or smelling a receiving blanket in your ninth month held powerful sway. You fantasized about the coming baby as you held the tiny booties, evidence of a life about to transform. Visualizing the new you as you rocked in the brand new, still unnecessary rocking chair, you smiled into your cradled arms. It was a beautiful way to come to understand your new role and responsibilities.

Fantasy helps you visualize how you will act and react in a new situation in a life you haven't yet lived. Visualization can feel silly sometimes or unnecessary. We think of it as juvenile behavior, like writing your first name with your boyfriend's last name a hundred times in high school study hall. Or we think of visualization as a mind game for athletes that is unnecessary for everyday achievements.

When an event is important to you, you are already visualizing, whether you consciously choose to or not. When you're nervous, you start thinking of all the what-ifs, imagining how everything could go wrong. Stress can cause a humiliating fantasy to play in your head over and over, like a bad tape. A conscious choice to visualize the positive can eject the bad tape and give you the result you are hoping for.

Even if you visualize the event, you may still have stage fright as you approach the big moment. It is perfectly normal to feel nervous. Even highly experienced speakers and actors feel nervous before a performance. Nervousness can be harnessed to give you energy and to project your passion. Remember, you've worked a long time to be ready for this moment, you've done all you can do, and now—thanks to positive visualization—you're ready to relax and give it your best shot. Mistakes are human, and can even be endearing, so don't berate yourself and rate your performance on one slip-up. If you've made a nervous mistake, close your eyes briefly and return in your mind to how you visualized it. Your earlier fantasy of this moment can put you back on track.

You can try another trick I've used when speaking to an audience. At the beginning of a speech, I need to calm myself so my words don't spill out too fast and make me seem nervous. I close my eyes briefly and picture my children. I silently tell the audience *I love you* just as I would to my kids. I stop to feel my child's hug or caress. When I open my eyes I feel loved in return. It's a good mind trick.

LABOR #36: YOU'RE DUE

Visualize your new life.

* Put on some low-key music, sit comfortably, and take time to fantasize about success and what's going to be yours as a result of your efforts.
* Use props and dress the part to help you feel your new role and responsibility.
* If you have an event at which you must perform, like a presentation or a speech, rehearse and prepare and visualize the best result.

The Nitty Gritty Is Not So Pretty

When you become pregnant, you feel as if you've been initiated into some secret society. Mothers everywhere smile at you and sidle up to you in public and at parties. They want to share your optimism and sense of purpose. But with the next breath, their memory darkens a bit and they utter *Better you than me.* Out come the truths about pregnancy and they aren't so pretty. They're the kinds of things only another mother knows and doesn't really like to think about. It may have taken us years to recoup our feminine mystique after any one of an endless array of potentially humiliating experiences—having to pee in a cup in the car in a traffic jam, getting busted for eating baby food, or realizing one sad morning that now your *shoes* don't fit.

And that's not to mention pregnancy insanity in which you indulged in every fear and insecurity known to womankind. What if my misspent youth is visited upon this poor baby? What if he looks like my Uncle Cyril? Fear of miscarriage, fear that something could be wrong with your body, fear that someone will accidentally touch your sensitive breasts and you'll explode. Fear that you'll throw up on national television. (What are the odds, unless you're Maria Shriver?)

These are just a few of the pregnancy taboos. Unpregnancy has taboos too, but they are mercifully different from the delightful array served up by pregnancy.

TOP TEN REASONS UNPREGNANCY IS BETTER THAN PREGNANCY

#10   You're not facing down months of wondering which unattractive symptoms are headed your way. Swollen ankles? Varicose veins? Stretch marks? Love handles? Morning Sickness?

#9   Maybe your breasts don't get bigger, but neither does your waistline, your thighs or your rear end! (Do I look like that from the back?)

#8   You can color your hair and drink diet sodas. And you can have a glass of wine—in public.

#7   You can sleep through the night.

#6   You may need new clothes but you're sure to like them better than maternity clothes.

#5   Your husband won't put on empathy weight.

#4   You don't have to name the " new you" after any funky relatives.

#3   Your pantyhose won't roll down your belly when you bend over.

#2   You can bend over.

#1   Labor and delivery refer to self-exploration tasks and takeout food.

So now you know you're not alone. These feelings of fear and self–doubt happen to everyone. You don't have to hide in a closet or take to your bed. Who can you call, who can you rely on to give you the straight poop? Your friends. Unpregnant women are everywhere. You can see the signs: they're animated, they're purposeful, and they're on a mission. They're happy to help, just as they're learning to ask for help and support.

It takes a lot of focus, control, and commitment to bring about a new life. You have the personal proof that you can do it: you can sustain a colossal effort for nine months and accommodate a new person in your life. Keep your eyes on the prize because this is your *life* we're talking about.

LESSON #9

nothing can stop you in the homestretch

There's no such thing as a *little* pregnant or so they say. But there is without a doubt a recognizable state in your ninth month called *very pregnant*. Everyone knows what that means and it quickly elicits the empathy it deserves. Have you ever met a pregnant woman in her ninth month who would gladly continue indefinitely? Waddling, huffing, puffing and trying desperately to sleep in an enormous nest of pillows somehow all begins to lose its appeal. (Translation: Shoot me now.)

As much as you want it to be over, you realize the escape route isn't easy either. Looming ever larger is the prospect of labor and delivery. (No translation necessary.)

Who would even go through with it, if given a choice? Who in her right mind would sign up for that amount of labor and pain? Yet when labor strikes you're pretty excited and in the beginning you feel prepared and ready to go. (We all know that in the eleventh hour that feeling of preparedness becomes one of the hollow promises you vow to avenge as soon as you *get this baby out of you*.)

As labor announces itself, you face the challenge of your *life*—with a positive attitude, excitement, confidence, and calm. Why? Well, what choice do you have?

This is precisely the Unpregnancy lesson. To win a big prize, to achieve a life-altering goal, or to bring a new life into its own is never going to be easy. Human beings would not be human if they didn't try to opt out of pain, exhaustion, fear, labor, risk, uncertainty . . . and birth pangs that register on the Richter scale.

Think about "overnight" success stories. One day her life took on dramatic changes and we all took notice of her, seemingly overnight. Her "birth" into our awareness was preceded by the most *labor*-intensive period in her life followed by a roller coaster ride beyond compare and ending with a new life she could never have imagined before entering the canal (dare we say *unbirth* canal?). Many lives have been forever altered in the unbirth canal: American Idol winners with their promised recording contracts, Olympic medalists,

Miss America, *Survivor* survivors, presidential candidates—all were relative unknowns when they began their labors. They threw their hats into the ring, entered the labor room, and delivered with great focused effort. Did it happen overnight? Only for the onlookers.

How do we get *there*? At the precipice of birth? As Unpregnant women, we've been in the labor room and survived. Barring a desire for another child, we're not marching down that road again. And with the awareness of how rough it can get, most of us would not choose the path of greatest resistance because it's unnatural.

Now, here's a personal labor story. (C'mon, you knew I'd have to share it eventually.) I never went into labor naturally, not for any of my three births (let me stop here and thank God for modern medicine). With my first baby, I was induced when I was two weeks late. Labor began but even after 15 hours of what they considered "productive" labor there was *zero* dilation. And my little girl hadn't descended. The doctors decided to insert a catheter, which was a little balloon designed to do the work of a baby's head by exerting pressure from the inside and causing initial dilation (up to 3 centimeters). The next day we started the Pitossin drip again, my water broke and I endured about 20 hours of labor before it was determined that the baby was destined to be born by C-section.

My point in sharing in such gory detail is that any success requires pressure. An absence of outside pressure on your performance will result in and absence of meaningful progress on your Unpregnancy goal, despite labor! You might even have endless labor. But without product and progress, is it worth it?

Many of us are afraid to take the last steps but have come so far that we're not willing to give up either. We live in a limbo, still seeming to pursue our goals, still thinking highly of ourselves as a result, but not actually getting there. Why? The next steps are out of our control—they're too risky, too painful, and too scary.

We stay in labor (*consider that for an instant*) even when we know it's going nowhere. But we're too worried to ask for help, too scared to commit more deeply, and too unsure of ourselves to make the leap into the unbirth canal.

All three of my children were finally born via C-section. With my second child, I was very committed to trying a V-Bac (Vaginal Birth after Cae-

205

sarean). When they took a sonogram of her at one week post–due date, the sonogram technician said *Hold still baby, I'm trying to measure your head.* I asked what the baby was doing and was told that she was moving her head back and forth in an attempt to fit into the birth canal. That was a deciding moment for me. I had felt her attempts for more than a week. We scheduled a C-section and she was born with contusions on her temples from trying to fit her head into my pelvic bone.

Again, why the gory detail? I never went into labor naturally and I'm told that if I hadn't received professional intervention, all three of my wonderful, zany children might have been stillborn because my birth canal could not accommodate them. Yet as the pregnancies progressed, they were only getting larger and the placenta, their lifeline, was sloughing off.

I know it's uncomfortable to think of a child being stillborn and I apologize to any readers for whom this term raises difficult memories. But my point here is that your dreams could be stillborn if you don't enter the unbirth canal, take the risks, get the support and help you need, and *push with every fiber of your being.* You have a window of opportunity during which your dream still has a lifeline and you have the love and professional support you need. Don't prolong your due date and ignore the signs that it's time to jump; if you do, your dreams might just die.

How does an Unpregnant woman get her baby/project to descend and exert itself on her world? How do we get to where *we must* go into labor, bringing forth the lives we dream of whether we want to or not?

What is our metaphoric Pitocin? Our C-section? How do we guarantee that our labors will deliver us to the goals we dream of achieving? Once again our pregnancy experiences give us the answers: pressure, timing, exertion, and professional intervention.

I'll take these one at a time, starting with **Pressure**. Just as I couldn't dilate without the pressure of a baby's head, it is fairly impossible to change your life without taking on some pressure. And if that's unappetizing, consider this: you have to create the pressure yourself! You need to approach each trimester and your entire Unpregnancy with an eye to where and when you must commit to things that will make your dreams a reality. There are ways to plan for appropriate, productive pressure, such as renting space, inviting a seminar audience to your house, setting up auditions, interviews, or deadlines with third parties, booking a date at an open mic, trying out for a show, seeking a grant or internship. Create a commitment that comes with an elevated expectation and therefore *pressure*. If you want these dates to happen within a certain trimester, then you have to plan them. Next, work backward and consider what you will need to do to in order to prepare for that commitment. Add those steps to your plan and schedule time for preparation and exploration.

If you build a better mousetrap, as the saying goes, they'll beat a path to your door. I don't think this is true in this day and age. If you build *and market* a better mousetrap, then maybe. You need to reach out and bring the world to you; only then will there be a demand for your mousetrap.

People used to ask me all the time how I could keep my focus when I worked from home. I'm as lazy as the next gal. My success as a marketing writer came from outside pressure. I had built my brand and business by being good, reliable and responsive. If I was working on a project, my phone rang all day. My email was full of pressure—things to read and respond to by a certain time, client conference calls and expectations. I wrote research and concept papers on what strategies would be most effective to raise awareness and sales of many different products. These musings were hundreds of pages long and very closely read and considered by marketing professionals who were weighing how to allocate millions of their marketing dollars to have the greatest impact on their bottom lines. As I worked at my computer for sometimes 20 hours at a stretch, my husband running ice chips in to me and mopping my brow, you can bet I was feeling outside pressure. (Otherwise, why do it?)

You need to create a group of people to whom you are committed, who expect you to achieve certain goals by a certain time. Find people to whom you are indebted—you've promised and you owe them material progress by a certain time and date. That kind of pressure will push you even when you don't yet feel the urge to push.

Timing is everything. Unpregnancy is nine months long for good reason. It's a pre-established length of time that we innately know we deserve. It's a time frame that our experience has proven to be productive. We've never had a bigger life change than a pregnancy and birth and that took precisely nine months. It is also a period of time that we have proven to ourselves we can endure with self-deprivation, labor, and hardship while maintaining grace under pressure, optimism, and even joy. Nine months will get the job done. A nine-month deadline gives you time to build the necessary infrastructure and outside pressure and the perfect timing to quit finessing, fiddling, and fretting over it—a delivery deadline. At nine months it is what it is—lovable, perfect, yours, *delivered*.

Exertion. You exert yourself by making a strong personal commitment to hard work, doing whatever it takes, and leaving behind petty concerns and road-blocks in order to give birth (and all that that implies) to your newborn you.

Professionals are a necessary component to your success. This is no time for Yankee pride, American individualism, or a retreat to the artist's garret. You cannot do it all and you will not change your life all by yourself. It will be your drive, your vision, and your *labor* that brings it to fruition, but at the end of labor you want and need people around you.

The reason Unpregnancy has two trimesters prior to conquering the public roles we aspire to is to ensure that the people we love will be with us when we give birth to that new life—that we are on solid ground with our-selves and with our family and friends. At this important milestone in our lives we want to be with and feel the love and support of those we love.

But we also need the professionals—the doctors, midwives, nurses (and don't forget the anesthesiologist!). We need relationships with professionals we trust to guide us safely through uncharted territory. Your Unpregnancy goal may require a lawyer, an accountant, a coach, an agent or a publicist. During my first pregnancy, we had moved out to the suburbs and I hadn't learned to drive yet. I had put off learning to drive for 12 years, but once pregnant I didn't think twice about finally hiring a driving teacher and get-ting my license. You need to schedule time to find the right providers and build a reliable relationship with each of them before your *un*birthday.

LABOR #37: APPLY PRESSURE

To build pressure, create a labor environment and bring the professionals you need into your life, you'll need a plan.

Make yourself 10 copies of the undated calendar chart below and fill in the dates of your Unpregnancy by consulting a standard calendar. Beginning from Day One, create the nine months of your Unpregnancy. The dates go in the squares in the upper left corner of each day. There are 280 days in your Unpregnancy (93 days per trimester plus your Unbirthday = 280 days). Now create an Unpregnancy countdown by writing the number 280 by the first day of your Unpregnancy and continuing backward till you reach #1—your Unbirthday. At number 187 (187 days left) be sure to mark that day as the beginning of your second trimester and at number 94 (94 days left) begin your third trimester. Plot the important events—the baby steps—for your goals and work backward to create your plan for building in the pressure, timing, exertion and professional support you need to get your urge to push.

TRIMESTER # _____

PRIMARY GOAL: _____

Monday	Tuesday	Wednesday	Thursday	Friday	Saturday	Sunday
____ (#)	____ (#)	____ (#)	____ (#)	____ (#)	____ (#)	____ (#)
____ (#)	____ (#)	____ (#)	____ (#)	____ (#)	____ (#)	____ (#)
____ (#)	____ (#)	____ (#)	____ (#)	____ (#)	____ (#)	____ (#)
____ (#)	____ (#)	____ (#)	____ (#)	____ (#)	____ (#)	____ (#)
____ (#)	____ (#)	____ (#)	____ (#)	____ (#)	____ (#)	____ (#)

IMPORTANT EVENTS

Trimester #	Trimester #	Trimester #	Trimester #
Goal:	Goal:	Goal:	Goal:
January	**April**	**July**	**October**
○	○	○	○
○	○	○	○
○	○	○	○
○	○	○	○
○	○	○	○
○	○	○	○
February	**May**	**August**	**November**
○	○	○	○
○	○	○	○
○	○	○	○
○	○	○	○
○	○	○	○
○	○	○	○
March	**June**	**September**	**December**
○	○	○	○
○	○	○	○
○	○	○	○
○	○	○	○
○	○	○	○
○	○	○	○

Deadline

In the marketing business if you're working on a project and the deadline approaches, it's time to start loving it. You have to give up nitpicking, starting over, or worse, not selling what you have. Any work—creative or otherwise— is simply a snapshot of a moment in time. It is the best you can do by a pre-ordained time given the circumstances. The time for changing things is over and the time for accepting has begun. Deadlines are a reality that creates pressure, but also relieves pressure. If you create a deadline for yourself, you have a time by which you must finish something or bring it to the next phase and a time at which you can let go. If you never have a deadline, you can rework a project endlessly as you aim for perfection.

Tell yourself: It is what it is. I've reached the deadline so I must release the work. Ding. Time to share my thoughts, ideas, and dreams with an audience. Is there work in your drawer, in your head, on your bedside table, or in a file on your computer? Do you have a drawing, an idea, something you're writing or planning that you have not yet shared with anyone else? Is there a plan or an idea that you are afraid to share because it doesn't seem ready?

1. Set yourself a deadline. Date _____

2. Plan a meeting or an event with more than one person—your audience—to share your work on that date.
    With whom _____

    ✔ Call a group or an individual and ask to meet *on* that date.

    ✔ Consider finding a less personal audience: an open mic night or a poetry or writers' reading group you can join or Toastmasters.

    ✔ If you feel you cannot meet that date due to circumstances beyond your control, proactively extend the deadline and re-establish the audience dates.

3. Don't beg off. On the scheduled date, let go of your work, share your idea—and sell it!

Your Due Date

However your baby is born—in a taxi or in a hospital, back labor or breach, natural, medicated, or Cesarean—you know you earned that baby, *your* baby. This simple attitude is an undeniable and overlooked gift of pregnancy and birth. You are at once grateful and overwhelmed at the miracle of birth while still feeling completely deserving. Blessed and deserving. Think about it. Those two feelings don't often go hand in hand. Often when we achieve what we have longed for and worked hard for, we still feel undeserving when it comes to pass. *It was no big deal. I was just lucky.* In fact, we find it difficult to internalize that our actions made it happen and we deserve the praise, the reward, the position we have worked to achieve.

This discrepancy between your actual achievements and your feelings of worthiness is called Imposter Syndrome, a syndrome that is widespread among high-achieving women. The syndrome, identified by psychologists Pauline Clance and Suzanne Imes, is a combination of three strongly held beliefs: you think you are a fake and are not as good as people seem to think and you are undeserving of the accolades and awards you earn; people are soon going to find out you're a fake; and any error could lead to unmasking you as a fraud, resulting in terrible consequences.

Despite external proof of your accomplishments—college degrees, awards, community achievements—you cannot internalize the experience and you therefore attribute it to luck, timing, or fooling others into thinking you are smarter or more capable than you know yourself to be. Each accomplishment, rather than mitigating doubts, intensifies the fear of being found out.

Imposter Syndrome does not have to be an all-or-nothing belief system. You might relate to some aspects of the syndrome and not others—e.g., you might be unable to accept a compliment, or shrink from taking deserved credit, or worry about being exposed. As a result, you overcompensate, cover up and work very hard to assure yourself that no one will be able to trip you up, turn you in and betray your secret to your supervisor. You might shy away from showing confidence in your work, fearing that any realistic acceptance of your intelligence will be perceived as braggadocio or as distasteful.

On another note, no employer, coworker or even committee cochair is likely to tell you that your overkill approach could be scaled back. No one else suffers from your Imposter Syndrome—they're happy to take advantage of your need to do more than your share.

No matter how unsure of yourself you are at work, even if you are a compulsive control freak and suffering from full-blown Imposter Syndrome, there was one time and place when it all fell away. When you accepted your baby into your arms and were promoted to the status of Mom, there was a peaceful acceptance of this achievement. You knew you earned it and you felt like the hero you were. The crucible of the birthing room removes any doubt about what you're due on your due date.

When it seems too good to be true and you're sure you didn't earn your place in the world, do a reality check. Question your doubts and try to come up with more positive and balanced thoughts. Remember the whole peace you felt when holding your newborn—a testimony to your effort, your due. Try to recapture that calm sense that you worked for it, you earned it, *you're due.*

- ✔ Re-read your Morning Journal to recall the emotions, events, and efforts you've come through to get where you are today.
- ✔ Look back at the plan you created, your important events list.
- ✔ Say aloud and internalize the fact that you identified these tasks, prioritized them, and achieved them.
- ✔ Your work brought you to where you are today.

Accept What Happens—Boy? Girl? Fame? Fortune?

Nine months is a long time, but it's relatively short when you consider the life transformation you're shooting for. Can you remember being shocked by how tiny your newborn baby was? She was needy, tiny, and perfect but far from finished.

Nine months is proven to be long enough to transform your life, but you'll still have a lot of work left to get it launched, established, and up and running.

What if you only achieve 80 percent of your goal? You've still come a long way, baby. *Once begun is half done,* as that great sage Mary Poppins said. As your Unbirthday arrives and even if you're not quite at goal, celebrate your progress, your vision, and your hard work to date. Think of your achievements to date like a low-birth-weight baby—she might have a fight ahead of her but she's still a miracle.

What if you are rocketing well past your expectation and suddenly you're living a life you never could have imagined? What you wanted was to express yourself and what you're finding is a huge audience wanting more of your self-expression.

Accept what happens. Accept that it is yours and you deserve it. Now take another step and acknowledge that it is yours to accept or reject. Stay true to your mission even if your success is diverting you from it. Don't scrap your mission to include your current circumstances. Try to capitalize on your current success to steer back toward what you know you truly want in your life.

Live your new life starting from your Unbirthday and know that you brought it about. You were in the right place at the right time, doing the hard work; you prepared for the opportunity and recognized it as something you wanted and deserved. All these factors that you created and prepared for added up to where you are now. Accept your fate. You are blessed and deserving.

LABOR #39: WORDS TO LIVE BY

Think about the words that you lived by in your Unpregnancy—your mantra, your inspirations, your goals. You're entering a new phase of your life now. What words will you choose to live by?

Get your new attitude engraved in stone so you know it is permanent. Garden and gift stores often sell inspiring word stones. If you can find the one word that is meaningful to you, the one that evokes your Unpregnancy experience and achievement, you can simply purchase it.

You can also choose to make a rock out of Sculpey or Fimo clay that can be baked until it is hard rock or made into a paperweight. Write your word in the clay while it is still soft and then bake your work into a permanent reminder of your acceptance of this newly born you. You could create multiple stones. What many seminar moms choose to do is put a word on each side of the stone. What I notice is that the words are often opposites. Sometimes a striving mom has to be reminded to work, sometimes to play. A reversible stone can help her see both sides of her effort.

Words should remind you of your effort and your ongoing mantra and encourage you to embrace all that you've become.

Persevere	Play	Accept	Joy	Seek
Peace	Loll	Visualize	Ambition	Achieve
Unpregnancy	Give	Conceive	Awe	Forgive
Awesome	Wisdom	Wait	Wonder	Recharge
Dream	Gestate	Blessed	Explore	Awaken
Build	Stand	Permission	Share	
Create	Grow	Sing	Find	

The Urge to Push

I've already confided my labor stories, so you know that the first time in my life I was blessed with the urge to push was in my Unpregnancy. From countless stories, I know this urge cannot be denied whether you're in a cab or your doctor is out of the room or your husband isn't there yet to witness the birth of your child. No matter how sane or reasonable the requests are for you to wait, you cannot. You push—it is your divine right, your entire reason for being—and you become the push.

And as you push you get whatever you need to facilitate pushing—you yell at your husband or order the hospital staff around. You try any position. Your surroundings fall away as your precepts and modesty are stripped from you (literally). Without apology, without hesitation, you push.

Metaphorically speaking, I have the urge to push. And you will, too. When you have a story to tell, it pushes for you; when you find a passion, it creates its own divine permission and urgency. Your environment falls away—you're not distracted by TV, politeness, social obligations, or unwarranted expectations and you become an environment of your own making. The people who surround you are there to help you and you trust them. You trust them not to judge. You trust them to help in any way they can. The situation is almost out of your control. It is a lesson of pregnancy and a blessing of Unpregnancy. Many of us would be critical of being pushy even when we feel truly passionate. We stop and question what people will think and we worry about our image. Being pushy is not a highly regarded personal attribute, but we all know it's sometimes necessary and sometimes unavoidable.

As I said, I have known the urge to push in my Unpregnancy.

JULIA'S JOURNAL

I am soooo very Unpregnant right now. I'm tired of the pace I've established for writing this book and overwhelmed by my weekly seminar attendees who expect a new lesson from me each week. I even half afraid I'll be exposed as a fraud even as I mail out new seminar invitations. I was waddling around feeling sorry for myself the other day and I realized what an Unpregnancy moment I was having. I wanted the labor to be over.

I didn't want to write this final chapter. Poor me—I wanted my "baby" without the push. But the passion I have for Unpregnancy and its impact on the women I met each week kept me going. It was the people around me who helped me overcome my momentary dread and P U S H!

You too are blessed with a vision and an instinct to push. Take a lesson from pregnancy. Push without regard to how that looks or seems to onlookers. Give birth to your vision, your dream, your newly born you.

Celebrate

Cue the chorus—you've arrived.

As you tick off your important events and arrive at not one but three life-changing goals, you've amazed yourself and everyone around you.

Think of who you were and who you've become.

It's graduation day and your Unbirthday is approaching. Contemplate what might be in your Unpregnancy yearbook. What pictures would sum up your experience? What awards might be given out? Most likely to succeed? Most changed since last year? Prom Queen? (Why not? You're in charge.) Who would have signed your yearbook? What would the people you met along the way have to say to you at this auspicious moment? "Good luck?" "Thanks for the memories?" Would they quote poetry? Popular songs? Who would send you roses, money, gifts, cards? How proud would your grandma be today?

LABOR #40: CELEBRATE

Today is your Unbirthday, so send yourself a greeting card. (And get yourself a gift card from your favorite store, restaurant or spa while you're at it. You deserve it.)

t3/checkup

If your goal is not pushing you forward, are you sure your dream is fueled by passion?

One of my seminar attendees ended Lesson #9 by thinking about being pushy. Her feeling was that she hated pushy people. It was as if they felt entitled or better than others. It was distasteful to her. Then she realized there were times in everyone's life when they're entitled to help and attention, like when you're having a baby, times when pushing is just right. She stopped and wrote a letter to the Oprah show about Unpregnancy, hoping to help me push. It was a touching and charming letter and a gesture I'll never forget. I had demanded that she be pushy and I hope that when the time comes she'll push on her own behalf, too. Imagine staying pregnant forever rather than facing the endgame. No one could or would do that. Remember waiting to go into labor? Sometimes it was a few days and sometimes it was weeks. As you "procrastinated," the pressure grew and people started phoning you daily.

If you're not feeling the pressure, something is not quite right.

✴ **Consider things in your environment that hold you back.**

✴ **Consider times you checked your first instinct because of what someone else might think or say.**

✴ **Who would criticize you for being pushy?**

✴ **How would you respond to a real or implied rebuke?**

  • It's the only way for this to happen.

  • If we don't push now, it won't happen.

  • I've got to push while I've got the help and attention of . . .

  • I'm sorry I'm pushing so hard, but soon we'll be done and then we'll have.

✴ **Check in at www.unpregnancy.com and share your pushing stories.**

bringing up baby

Self-development is a higher duty than self-sacrifice.
— ELIZABETH CADY STANTON

Pregnancy—it was the best of times. It was the worst of times. Pregnancy was a time of great challenge, courage, hopefulness and duty. As we've explored, it gave us many gifts and lessons, such as adversity, on which to strike character, and trials over which to triumph. It made us stronger and weaker at the same time. Your growing (or grown) child reminds you of your duty to yourself and to the next generation to live your best possible life and give them your best possible gift. Now is the time for your Unpregnancy.

Every woman who has ever been pregnant and raised a child has an enormously rich experience to draw upon and offer the world. Don't allow yourself or others to belittle this know-how. It is there for you. Take it, feed it, and allow it to grow into everything you've been missing in your life. We all take our own experiences, memories and outcomes from a pregnancy. We can each draw on the individual and the collective lessons learned to get the life we want today for ourselves.

Taking back the time, structure and process of pregnancy gives us each nine months and three trimesters during which to strive. It's a long period of dedicated effort and effective labor. But as our own life experience shows us, it is not too long and not unendurable. Unpregnancy's gift of time and ever-increasing intensity of expectation is what we can gain from our pregnancies past. Our pregnancy can fuel our efforts by giving us back memories, insights and schooling in human nature, nurture and our own family/work/community dynamics. What we observed in pregnancy we reclaim in Unpregnancy.

in due time

NINE MONTHS, THREE TRIMESTERS, LABOR, AND DELIVERY

Unpregnancy is structured in three trimesters. As in a pregnancy, trimesters help you measure growth and clock expectations. You began with a small embryo that perhaps only you knew about—a seed of something big to come. So begins an Unpregnancy. It starts with an idea, something small and personal that foretells a big life change. Like a child conceived, your Unpregnancy starts with you and yet could eventually grow well beyond your current life circumstance.

These truths—these lessons learned in pregnancy—we hold to be self-evident. You have reclaimed this basic self-knowledge to form the basis of your Unpregnancy—nine months, nine lessons just for you. Review the lessons and think about how each applies to you, both in your past and your future. How can it help you overcome both internal and external obstacles and move yourself toward the light? As thoughts occur to you, jot them down in the right column so you can preserve the insights and ideas that occur to you as you reread the lessons.

FIRST TRIMESTER/SELF

Put Yourself First: Begin with yourself—your health, your spirit, your well-being. Whether you need exercise or creativity or an entrepreneurial challenge, begin with what you need and nourish that first.

Keep a Morning Journal to help you be in touch with what matters to you and what is missing in your life. Be true to your own need regardless of who else's needs might have to take a backseat. You're not resigning as head chef and bottle washer, but you're accepting applications for part-time help. You'll find ways to change people's expectations of you and fit in just what you need. If you've taken the time to identify what you truly want, your time spent pursuing it will become addictive. Like the developing fetus in the womb, it will press and grow and make its own room in your life.

You'll Never Be Alone Again

Even as you realize you'll never be alone again, you learn to develop that truism into something that supports your way of life and your way of thinking and guides you in decision making that won't compromise what you hold dearest—your friends and family and your relationships. You'll see how to commit to a course of action without conflict or compromise within the context of your real life. On the flip side of family/friend obligation, you'll see the true family/friend opportunity—connectivity. Empower yourself to capitalize on the asset you've built in good faith—your network.

Your thoughts

Only You Can Do This

Pregnancy gave us something bigger than ourselves (no pun intended) to believe in and contribute to. Pregnancy gave us a mission with a life force. All our decisions became clear-cut. Finding a mission for your life (and it's there, as sure as a prenatal heartbeat) will act as a divining rod for your decision making and time allocation. Your mission will provide you goals and policies that will help you allocate time and resources for success. You must do this. Only you can.

Your thoughts

You Are Great, with Child

We take from our children what they offer so eagerly and remember to partake of the mood-altering substances they were weaned on: joy, positivity, gratitude, wonder and awe. We need to remember that we deserve pure joy, wonder and awe. And only positivity will get us there. Framing your goal and mantra in yes-words and positive results can be mood-altering, quite literally.

Your thoughts

SECOND TRIMESTER/LOVE

In a Family Way: After a hiatus from the motherly focus on others, you'll be refreshed. Look to help spread your sense of joy and purpose with your friends and loved ones. After three months of self-awareness and carving out time and opportunity to be true to yourself, you'll be better equipped to help your loved ones (perhaps better equipped than you've been in years). You'll be serving them a new and exciting dish—a mission of their own and self-empowerment.

You're Gestating

(Everything Else Can Wait)

When did we as human beings become human doers? When you were pregnant, you were content to just be and let your body achieve the doing. Your value wasn't linked to what you accomplished in a day. You need time to gestate. Get off the hamster wheel of futility and conceive a new life. (When else are you going to do it? This is your life.)

Your thoughts

You Don't Know What to Expect

As soon as you tell anyone you're pregnant, expectations shift. People are excited for you or are worried for you. They expect different things from you whether or not they say so. You have different expectations, too. For a brief time, all your expectations are in play. You renegotiate exchanges in every relationship. You ask for help, say no when you're overtired, listen to and respect your own needs. Once Unpregnant, you can do that any day of the week. Suddenly, you have the power to expect change in your life!

Your thoughts

Napping Is Not a Crime

It takes time to grow into the new you. You need to give yourself permission to nap, ask for help, unload onerous tasks, ignore others—act the Unpregnant diva! Often, as soon as we take a break or neglect a job, we are chastised and filled with fear, guilt, doubt, or despair. Pregnancy can help us recall a time when we napped without recourse. We unapologetically shifted our energies into the pregnancy just as you will now with your Unpregnancy. The nine-month effort is difficult but worth it; it's hard work for a short, sustained time, with life-altering results!

Your thoughts

THIRD TRIMESTER/WORK

You're Showing! In your third trimester you should be well on your way to developing success and a big difference in your life. Like a big belly in the ninth month, it is obvious to everyone, even strangers. You've created a healthy foundation within yourself and at home. You're ready to build a new and exciting public role for yourself. Map out what it would take to get a new job, take on an exciting challenge, or fulfill the dream of a lifetime.

Is Mother Nature Kidding Me?

It is natural, even if far from normal, to give birth. To your surprise, the infrastructure was there, the path was blazed, and the impossible made possible. It is equally natural to nurture dreams and ambitions. It is nature's way of promoting excellence and growth in our generation and the next. To find our calling and then not pursue it goes against nature.

Pregnancy also gave us new respect for our natural bodies, whatever shape or size, and allowed us to shift our focus elsewhere. Post-pregnancy we lost all ambition as our days became a blur of nursing and nurturing. This lesson teaches us to reconnect with our natural selves and ambitions.

Your thoughts

Keep Your Eyes on the Prize

Pregnancy was not a passive thing. You were pregnant every day and in every way. Even as you worked to maintain normalcy and meet expectations, you invested an enormous amount of time and energy into learning about pregnancy and birth. You were in it to winit! You dedicated yourself—all your resources—to ensure a successful outcome. Your whole life leaned into it.

Unpregnancy deserves a similar level of focus, intensity, and resources to get you the new life you dream of.

Your thoughts

Nothing Can Stop You in the Homestretch

In the end, you have to push. You would have done anything to have your baby magically and without pain or inconvenience, but it never happens that way. You've got to push. Time to shoulder the responsibility and make it happen. You can do this.

Your thoughts

no small feat

The pitter patter of little feet is behind you and ahead are great feats. Set your sights high. Track your progress and grow into your new role. You know you can do it because you've done it before.

I have three children. In my estimation, that entitles me to three Unpregnancies, three nine-month life cycles to devote wholeheartedly to me and my life's pursuits. I came by my first Unpregnancy by accident and in the process I discovered in myself a life I could be proud of and enjoy living. If I had chosen a fourth pregnancy instead, I would have a four- or five-year-old now, a little boy or girl who would delightfully consume me. I would revel in this precious life and its new point of view, its new ideas, thoughts, comments, talents, and opportunities. Since we were not ready to parent another baby, I chose to pour my loving energies into an Unpregnancy—into myself. I've come to embrace that selfishness. I took nine months to focus on and expand myself. With the devotion of a new mother, I chose to delight in myself, my new point of view, my new ideas, thoughts, comments, talents, and opportunities.

I know my expanding outlook gave everyone in my family a wider perspective. I brought home joy, ambition, and greater opportunity. Each Unpregnancy put me in fast forward into the life I now feel privileged to call my own.

My Accomplishments	My First Unpregnancy	My Second Unpregnancy
T1/Self	I lost 50 pounds.	I quit drinking alcohol.
T2/Love	I attended a marriage seminar with my husband, took a cruise together, and worked with each child to redesign his or her room.	Took my kids on a cross-country trip in a 1985 RV and wrote a book together on our return— *RV There Yet? – A Cross Country Cautionary Tale.*
T3/Work	I took my skill set into a a new arena and got a community pool built. I attended an excellent career seminar and began to consider how to transition from marketing to writing and speaking. I developed and lived my first Unpregnancy.	I assembled my first ever Unpregnancy seminar and hosted a group of women weekly and wrote this book.

My third Unpregnancy is yet to come. Who knows what I'll try (and achieve) in my third? I'm currently nurturing the small wonder that was borne of my second Unpregnancy. I'm writing its last chapter. It is keeping me up nights, filling my thoughts and my heart. I'm feeding and bonding with the new me, an author and a speaker. She's different, but still me.

otherhood

I'm raising a big life to which I owe myself everything I can give. Sometimes it is overwhelming and sometimes I feel undeserving. I look at my three children and fret about how to raise them or what to do next for them. I manage and plan. I am raising them with all the care and love I have to give. It's full-tilt motherhood.

Who knows where your Unpregnancy will take you? Bite off more than you can chew. Try and try again. Unpregnancy, like pregnancy, builds character and enriches your life immeasurably. It teaches you everything you need to metamorphose and change your life forever.

You're past due. Labor and delivery are scary but unavoidable. You're filled with excitement and trepidation yet unwaveringly focused. All your thoughts, all your actions will lead to achieving your goals.

Everything you do (and don't do) is guided by the task before you. You save your strength, you pamper yourself, you visualize and consider.

Sometimes your mind pushes through labor and delivery and you think about the reward—the baby, your baby. The book contract, "the call," the grant, the award: Otherhood—a moment in your ninth month when you just know.

Your Otherhood approaches. Like coming home with your baby for the first time, it is momentous yet familiar.

This is a new life but still yours. As my children grow and thrive, so does my new life. It's getting BIG. BIGGER. I'm filled with love and pride. I did this. I am great, with child.

Your Unbirthday approaches. You're due.

Unpregnancy. It is the best of times.

acknowledgments

This book has had many midwives, and I'd like to acknowledge and thank the many, many people who have helped me bring this brain-child into the world. I'd like to thank Jennifer Kasius, my editor, designer Susan Van Horn and Craig Herman, and the rest of the Running Press staff whose input was invaluable in this process to shape and strengthen this book. I'd also like to thank my agents Joëlle Delbourgo and Jennifer Repo. There have been many others who have helped me in my labors! I'd like to thank my friend Liza Dawson who helped me shape my personal manifesto into a book. Fawn Germer, and Paul O'Hallorhan helped me connect with the right agent. Thanks for encouragement go to Elizabeth Roberts, Pamela Satran, Carole Hyatt, Debra Galant and Alice Dark. Of course my husband Adam Philips and our three children Sophie, Lucy and Freddy were essential to the character-building experience that motherhood became. Finally, I can't help but feel grateful to the very first group of moms who came to my house to each week, and worked on changing their lives, using my Labors and chapters. Thanks to: Elise Blatt, Kristen Carlberg, Kathy Kogut, Julie Raskin, Joy Taylor, Patty Topping, Kathy Weissenberger and Julie Zichelli. They've all gone on to do such wonderful things with their lives, that I could see the importance of bringing *Motherhood to Otherhood* to all moms.